# PRACTICAL INFORMATION

CONCERNING

# THE PUBLIC DEBT

OF THE

# UNITED STATES,

WITH THE

# NATIONAL BANKING LAWS.



**SECOND EDITION.**

---

BY
WILLIAM A. RICHARDSON,
SECRETARY OF THE TREASURY.

---

WASHINGTON, D. C.:
W. H. & O. H. MORRISON,
LAW PUBLISHERS AND BOOKSELLERS.
1873.

# CONTENTS.

## PART I.

### Practical Information Concerning the Public Debt.

CONTENTS.

# PART II.

THE NATIONAL BANKING LAWS OF THE UNITED STATES, WITH NOTES AND REFERENCES TO THE DECISIONS OF THE COURTS AND OPINIONS OF THE ATTORNEYS GENERAL THEREON.

---

# PART I.

## PRACTICAL INFORMATION CONCERNING THE PUBLIC DEBT OF THE UNITED STATES.

# CHAPTER 1.

## BONDED DEBT NOT MATURED, PAYABLE IN COIN.

| Title of Loan. | Interest. | | Amount Outstanding April 1, 1873. | | | Redeemable after— | Payable. |
|---|---|---|---|---|---|---|---|
| | Rate. | Payable. | Registered. | Coupon. | Total. | | |
| 1. Funded Loan of 1881. | 5 | Feb., May, Aug., Nov. | $128,809,750 00 | $71,190,250 00 | $200,000,000 00 | May 1, 1881 | |
| 2. Consols of 1868, or 5-20's of 1868. | 6 | Jan., July, | 14,155,500 00 | 24,472,900 00 | 38,628,400 00 | July 1, 1873 | July 1, 1888 |
| 3. Consols of 1867, or 5-20's of 1867. | 6 | Jan., July, | 90,902,100 00 | 224,776,100 00 | 315,678,200 00 | July 1, 1872 | July 1, 1887 |
| 4. Consols of 1865, or 5-20's of 1865. | 6 | Jan., July, | 58,807,000 00 | 148,784,150 00 | 207,591,150 00 | July 1, 1870 | July 1, 1885 |
| 5. Five-twenties of 1865. | 6 | May, Nov. | 36,454,250 00 | 119,199,600 00 | 155,653,850 00 | Nov. 1, 1870 | Nov. 1, 1885 |
| 6. Five-twenties of June, 1864. | 6 | May, Nov. | 32,707,750 00 | 34,413,000 00 | 67,120,750 00 | Nov. 1, 1869 | Nov. 1, 1884 |
| 7. Five-twenties of March, 1864. | 6 | May, Nov. | 2,298,000 00 | ........ | 2,298,000 00 | Nov. 1, 1869 | Nov. 1, 1884 |
| 8. Ten-forties.......... | 5 | Mar., Sept. | 140,026,300 00 | 54,541,000 00 | 194,567,300 00 | Mar. 1, 1874 | Mar. 1, 1904 |
| 9. Loan of 1863, or 6's of 1881. | 6 | Jan., July, | 53,495,450 00 | 21,504,550 00 | 75,000,000 00 | Jun 30, 1881 | |
| 10. Five-twenties of 1862. | 6 | May, Nov. | 30,797,350 00 | 233,292,800 00 | 264,090,150 00 | May 1, 1867 | May 1, 1882 |
| 11. Loan of July and Aug., 1861, or 6's of 1881. | 6 | Jan., July, | 125,513,550 00 | 63,807,800 00 | 189,321,350 00 | Jun 30, 1881 | |
| 12. Oregon War Debt. | 6 | Jan., July, | ........ | 945,000 00 | 945,000 00 | ........ | July 1, 1881 |
| 13. Loan of Feb., 1861, or 6's of 1881. | 6 | Jan., July, | 13,759,000 00 | 4,656,000 00 | 18,415,000 00 | ........ | Dec. 31, 1880 |
| 14, Loan of 1858........ | 5 | Jan., July, | 6,045,000 00 | 13,955,000 00 | 20,000,000 00 | Jan. 1, 1874 | |
| Aggregate........ | ...... | ........ | 733,771,000 00 | 1,015,538,150 00 | 1,749,309,150 00 | | |

Outstanding loans not matured.

The bonds of the United States, of which both the principal and interest are payable in coin, now outstanding, and neither called in for payment nor fully matured, are known under fourteen distinct titles, representing that number of different loans, which are kept entirely separate on the books of the Treasury Department. Coupon bonds may be exchanged for registered stock either in the same or other denominations, and mutilated, defaced, or indorsed bonds may be returned and clean new bonds obtained therefor; but all such exchanges must be in the same loan, and the bonds of one issue can never be converted into nor combined with those of either of the others.

The table at the head of this chapter gives the titles, amounts, times of payment of principal and interest, and the rate of interest of all such loans, in chronological order, beginning with that of the latest date and extending back to that of the earliest issue, the loan of 1858; a full explanation of each of which is contained in the following pages of this chapter, under numbers referring to the loans as set forth in the table.

1.

### The Funded Loans.

Refunding act of 1870.

To enable the Secretary of the Treasury to fund at a lower rate of interest that part of the national debt represented by the five-twenty bonds, bearing six per cent. interest, Congress passed the following act:

AN ACT TO AUTHORIZE THE REFUNDING OF THE NATIONAL DEBT.

*Be it enacted by the Senate and House of Representatives of the United States of America in Congress assembled,*

That the Secretary of the Treasury is hereby authorized to issue, in a sum or sums not exceeding in the aggregate two hundred million dollars—

Bonds at 5 per cent. interest.

Coupon or registered bonds of the United States, in such form as he may prescribe, and of denominations of fifty dollars, or some multiple of that sum, redeemable in coin of the present standard value, at the pleasure of the United States, after ten years from the date of their issue, and bearing interest, payable semi-annually, in such coin, at the rate of five per cent. per annum;

Also a sum or sums not exceeding in the aggregate three hundred million dollars of like bonds, the same in all respects, but payable at the pleasure of the United States, after fifteen years from the date of their issue, and bearing interest at the rate of four and a half per cent. per annum; At 4½ per cent.

Also a sum or sums not exceeding in the aggregate one thousand million dollars of like bonds, the same in all respects, but payable at the pleasure of the United States, after thirty years from the date of their issue, and bearing interest at the rate of four per cent. per annum; all of which said several classes of bonds and the interest thereon shall be exempt from the payment of all taxes or duties of the United States, as well as from taxation in any form by or under State, municipal, or local authority; and the said bonds shall have set forth and expressed upon their face the above specified conditions, and shall, with their coupons, be made payable at the Treasury of the United States. At 4 per cent. Exempt from taxation.

But nothing in this act, or in any other law now in force, shall be construed to authorize any increase whatever of the bonded debt of the United States. Debt not to be increased.

SEC. 2. *And be it further enacted*, That the Secretary of the Treasury is hereby authorized to sell and dispose of any of the bonds issued under this act, at not less than their par value for coin, and to apply the proceeds thereof to the redemption of any of the bonds of the United States outstanding and known as five-twenty bonds, at their par value, or he may exchange the same for such five-twenty bonds, par for par; but the bonds hereby authorized shall be used for no other purpose whatsoever. Bonds, how sold and issued.

And a sum not exceeding one-half of one per cent. of the bonds herein authorized is hereby appropriated to pay the expense of preparing, issuing, advertising, and disposing of the same.

SEC. 3. *And be it further enacted*, That the payment of any of the bonds hereby authorized, after the expiration of the said several terms of ten, fifteen, and thirty years, shall be made in amounts to be determined from time to time by the Secretary of the Treasury, at his discretion, the bonds so to be paid to be distinguished and described by the dates and numbers, beginning for each successive payment with the bonds of each class last dated and numbered, of the time of which intended payment or redemption the Secretary of the Treasury shall give public notice, and the interest on the particular bonds so selected at any time to be paid shall cease at the expiration of three months from the date of such notice. How called in for payment.

SEC. 4. [*Authorizes the Secretary to call in for payment the five-twenty bonds.*] *See Chapter V.*

SEC. 5. [*Provides for the issue of coin certificates for gold deposits. Expired by limitation.*]

SEC. 6. [*Relates to the sinking fund.*] *See Chapter VI.*

*Approved July* 14, 1870.

Five hundred millions 5 per cent.

The amount of bonds which may be issued of the five per cent. loan is increased to five hundred millions dollars, and the interest of any portion of the bonds of the funded loans may be paid quarter-annually, by the following act:

AN ACT TO AMEND AN ACT ENTITLED "AN ACT TO AUTHORIZE THE REFUNDING OF THE NATIONAL DEBT."

*Be it enacted by the Senate and House of Representatives of the United States of America in Congress assembled,*

Interest payable quarterly.

That the amount of bonds authorized by the act approved July fourteen, eighteen hundred and seventy, entitled "An act to authorize the refunding of the national debt," to be issued, bearing five per centum interest per annum, be, and the same is, increased to five hundred millions of dollars, and the interest of any portion of the bonds issued under said act, or this act, may, at the discretion of the Secretary of the Treasury, be made payable quarter-yearly: *Provided, however,* That this act shall not be construed to authorize any increase of the total amount of bonds provided for by the act to which this act is an amendment.

*Approved January* 20, 1871.

Under these acts there are three loans called "FUNDED LOANS," from the object of the law, to refund the national debt at a lower rate of interest, differing from each other only in the rates of interest and in the times after which they may be redeemed, which latter difference gives to each its distinctive title.

Funded, of 1881, 5 per cent.

The "FUNDED LOAN OF 1881" is redeemable at the pleasure of the United States after the first day of May, A. D. 1881, and bears interest at the rate of five per cent. per annum, payable quarterly.

—of 1886, 4½ per cent.

The "FUNDED LOAN OF 1886," provided for by law but not yet issued, is redeemable at the pleasure of the United States after the first day of May, A. D. 1886, and bears interest at the rate of four and a half per cent. per annum, payable quarterly.

The "FUNDED LOAN OF 1901," provided for by law but not yet issued, is redeemable at the pleasure of the United States after the first day of May, 1901, and bears interest at the rate of four per cent. per annum, payable quarterly.

—of 1901, 4 per cent.

The bonds of each of these issues, unlike those of any other loan ever issued by the Government, express upon their face, in accordance with the requirements of the law, applicable to these bonds alone, that the principal and interest are "payable in coin of the standard value of the United States, July 14, 1870," the date of the passage of the act, and that both are "exempt from payment of all taxes or duties of the United States, as well as from taxation in any form by or under State, municipal, or local authority."

Payable in coin.

Exempt from taxation.

The interest is payable quarterly, on the first days of February, May, August, and November, in each year; and that upon registered bonds is sent by checks directly to the holders of the bonds at any post-office address designated by them, in this country or in Europe. Coupon bonds all bear date May 1, 1871, and both the coupon and registered bonds are designated on their face "FUNDED LOAN OF 1881," or "OF 1886," or "OF 1901," with the rate of interest.

Interest.

Two hundred millions dollars of the five per cents. have already been negotiated; but as yet none of the four per cents. and four and a half per cents. have been issued.

These are the only loans now offered for sale by the Government. All others, having long since been closed, are being reduced as rapidly as the surplus revenues, the money obtained from the sale of the new bonds, and the coin in the Treasury, will permit.

Only loan now offered by Government.

The reduction of the public debt for three years last past has been at the rate of about a hundred millions dollars a year; and the proceeds of the sale of the Funded Loan, which can be used only to redeem the five-twenty bonds and not to increase the public debt, has still further reduced the amount of bonds bearing six per cent. interest.

The bonds are all printed on the distinctive paper adopted by the Secretary of the Treasury, and manufactured under the supervision of the Department, as described in Chapter III.

Bonds are printed on distinctive paper.

The denominations are $50, $100, $500, $1,000, $5,000, and $10,000 coupon and registered bonds, and $20,000 and $50,000 also of the registered bonds.

## 2, 3, 4.

## CONSOLS OF 1865, OF 1867, AND OF 1868;

or

## FIVE-TWENTIES OF 1865, OF 1867, AND OF 1868.

Consols. Acts of authorization.

The act of Congress of March 3, 1865, (chapter 77,) authorized the Secretary of the Treasury to borrow on the credit of the United States any sums not exceeding in the aggregate six hundred millions of dollars, and to issue therefor bonds or treasury notes, the bonds to be in denomination not less than fifty dollars, and made payable at any period not more than forty years from date, or made redeemable and payable, as aforesaid, as might be expressed upon their face, with interest payable semi-annually. The act provided that the principal or interest, or both, of the bonds and treasury notes might be made payable in coin, or in lawful money; that the rate of interest, when payable in coin, should not exceed six per cent., and that the rates and character of interest should be expressed on all such bonds or treasury notes.

Origin of the application of the name of CONSOLS, to.

The act still further provided, that the treasury notes should be made convertible into any bonds authorized by the act; that any treasury notes or other obligations *bearing interest*, issued under any act of Congress, might, at the discretion of the Secretary of the Treasury, and with the consent of the holder, be converted into any description of said bonds; and that the bonds so authorized should not be considered a part of said six hundred millions. This provision for conversion was extended by act of April 12, 1866, (chapter 39,) so that the Secretary was authorized to receive any treasury notes or other obligations issued under any act of Congress, *whether bearing interest or not*, in exchange for any description of said bonds. The conversion or consolidation of other outstanding obligations into these loans gave to them the titles of CONSOLS, as they are called in the Treasury Department; but being redeemable at the pleasure of the Government after five years, and payable in twenty years from the date of issue, they are better known in the market as FIVE-TWENTIES of the different years of issue—1865, 1867, and 1868.

Also called five-twenties.

Under the provisions of the two acts above mentioned, for the conversion of treasury notes and other obligations, these issues of bonds were made and designated—

CONSOLS OF 1865, OR FIVE-TWENTIES OF 1865, which bear date July 1, 1865, became redeemable at the pleasure of the Government after July 1, 1870, and will be payable July 1, 1885. The amount issued was $332,998,950.

Consols of 1865.

CONSOLS OF 1867, OR FIVE-TWENTIES OF 1867, which bear date July 1, 1867, became redeemable at the pleasure of the Government after July 1, 1872, and will be payable July 1, 1887. The amount issued was $379,602,350.

—of 1867.

CONSOLS OF 1868, OR FIVE-TWENTIES OF 1868, which bear date July 1, 1868, became redeemable at the pleasure of the Government July 1, 1873, and will be payable July 1, 1888. The amount issued was $42,539,350.

—of 1868.

The bonds of these loans are all designated on their face with the words: "CONSOLIDATED DEBT, ISSUED UNDER ACT OF CONGRESS APPROVED MARCH 3D, 1865;" "REDEEMABLE AFTER FIVE AND PAYABLE TWENTY YEARS FROM DATE;" and "IN GOD IS OUR TRUST."

Bonds, how designated.

The interest is at the rate of six per cent. per annum, payable semi-annually, January 1 and July 1, in each year.

Interest, when payable.

Denominations: $50, $100, $500, and $1,000 coupon and registered bonds, and also $5,000 and $10,000 registered.

Denomination.

5.

## FIVE-TWENTIES OF 1865.

Of the six hundred millions of bonds authorized by the act of March 3, 1865, chapter 77, and the act of April 12, 1866, chapter 39, (under which the consols were issued by conversion of other obligations,) there were sold for money

Five-twenties of 1865.

Title of loan. and issued, $203,327,250, entitled, from the time after which they might be redeemed—five years—and the time of becoming payable—twenty years—and the date of their issue, Interest. "FIVE-TWENTIES OF 1865." Like the consols they bear interest at the rate of six per cent. per annum, and are redeemable When redeemable and payable. at the pleasure of the Government after five years and payable in twenty years from date, but unlike them, bear date November 1, 1865, and have the interest payable May 1 and November 1, in each year. They are designated on Designated. their face by the words "REDEEMABLE AFTER FIVE, AND PAYABLE TWENTY YEARS FROM DATE, and "ACT OF MARCH 3D, 1865." Denominations: $50, $100, $500, and $1,000 coupon and registered bonds, and also $5,000 and $10,000 registered.

For more full explanations of the provisions of the acts under which this loan was negotiated, *see "Consols," page* 12.

6.

## FIVE-TWENTIES OF JUNE, 1864.

Five-twenties of June, 1864. The act of June 30, 1864, chapter 172, authorized the Secretary of the Treasury to borrow, from time to time, on the credit of the United States, four hundred millions of dollars, and to issue therefor coupon or registered bonds, redeemable at the pleasure of the Government after any period not less than five nor more than thirty years, or, if deemed expedient, made payable at any period not more than forty years from date, and bearing interest, *in coin*, at the rate of six per cent. per annum, payable semi-annually.

Bonds issued. The amount issued was $125,561,300, in coupon and registered bonds, of $50, $100, $500, and $1,000, and also in registered bonds of $5,000 and $10,000, bearing date Redeemable. November 1, 1864, redeemable at the pleasure of the United States after the 31st day of October, 1869, and payable on Interest. the 1st day of November, 1884, with interest from the 1st day of November, 1864, inclusive, payable on the 1st day of May and November in each year.

Designation of bonds. These bonds are designated on their face, "SIX PER CENT. LOAN, UNDER ACT OF JUNE 30, 1864," and "REDEEMABLE AFTER

FIVE, AND PAYABLE TWENTY YEARS FROM DATE." The loan derives its title from the time after which it might be redeemed—five years—and the time of becoming payable—twenty years—with the month and year of the act of authorization. Title of loan.

7.

## Five-twenties of March, 1864.

This small loan, originally of $3,882,500, was issued under the same act as the ten-forty loan, approved March 3, 1864, chapter 17, of that year, for the balance of the two hundred millions not taken up in ten-forty bonds. The act provided that the bonds should bear date March 1, 1864, or any subsequent period; should be redeemable at the pleasure of the Government after any period not less than five years, and payable at any period not more than forty years from date, *in coin*, and of such denominations as might be found convenient, not less than fifty dollars, bearing interest not exceeding six per cent. a year, payable annually on bonds not over one hundred dollars, and semi-annually on all others, *in coin*. Act of authorization.

The title is derived from the time after which they might be redeemed—five years—and the time of becoming payable—twenty years—with the month and year of the passage of the act of authorization; and the face of the bonds bears the words, "REDEEMABLE AFTER FIVE, AND PAYABLE TWENTY YEARS FROM DATE," and "ACT OF MARCH 3, 1864." Title and designation.

There are no coupon bonds of this issue. The registered bonds are made redeemable at the pleasure of the United States after the 31st day of October, 1869, and payable on the 1st day of November, 1884, with interest at six per cent. per annum, payable semi-annually, on the 1st days of May and November in each year. Denominations: $100, $500, $1,000, and $5,000. Bonds all registered. Redeemable and payable. Interest.

8.

## Ten-forties,

Issued under the act of March 3, 1864, chapter 17, as were the "five-twenties of March, 1864." Ten-forties.

Title. It is the only loan ever issued with the provision that it might be redeemed in ten, and made payable in forty years from date, and takes its title from that fact.

Designation. The bonds are designated on the face "FIVE PER CENT. LOAN, UNDER ACT OF MARCH 3D, 1864," and "REDEEMABLE AFTER TEN, PAYABLE FORTY YEARS FROM DATE."

Denomination. They are of the denomination of $50, $100, $500, and $1,000, registered and coupon, and also $5,000 and $10,000 registered, and are made redeemable at the pleasure of the United States after the 28th day of February, 1874, and payable on the 1st day of March, 1904, with interest at five per cent. per annum, payable on the 1st day of March and September in each year, except that upon the $50 and $100 bonds it is payable annually on the 1st day of March.

Redeemable and payable.

Interest.

Amount. The whole amount issued was $196,117,300.

## 9.

## LOAN OF 1863;
or
## SIXES OF 1881.

Act of authorization. The act of March 3, 1863, chapter 73, section 1, authorized the Secretary of the Treasury to borrow from time to time, on the credit of the United States, not exceeding nine hundred millions of dollars, and to issue therefor coupon or registered bonds, payable at the pleasure of the Government after such periods as might be fixed by the Secretary, not less than ten nor more than forty years from date, *in coin*, and at such denominations, not less than fifty dollars, as he might deem expedient, bearing interest, *in coin*, at the rate of six per cent. per annum, payable on bonds not exceeding $100 annually, and on all others semi-annually. The act of June 30, 1864, chapter 172, limited the amount to be issued to seventy-five millions, then already advertised.

Title. The title of this loan on the books of the Treasury Department is "LOAN OF 1863," being the only one of that year; but as the bonds bear six per cent. interest, and may be redeemed in 1881, they are commonly called in the market "SIXES OF 1881." There are, however, two other loans, commonly called, also, for the same reason, "SIXES OF 1881," but distinguished by the years of their respective issue.

Designation of bonds.

The certificates and bonds bear on the face this designation: "TREASURY DEPARTMENT, ACT OF MARCH 3D, 1863," by which they may be distinguished from other sixes of 1881.

Bonds issued. Redeemable. Interest.

The whole seventy-five millions were issued in registered and coupon bonds of $50, $100, $500, and $1,000, and in registered also of $5,000 and $10,000, redeemable after the 30th day of June, 1881, with interest at six per cent. per annum, payable on the 1st days of January and July in each year, and are still outstanding.

## 10.

## FIVE-TWENTIES OF 1862.

Acts of authorization.

Section 2, chapter 33, of the act of February 25, 1862, authorized the Secretary of the Treasury, in order to fund the treasury notes and floating debt, to issue, on the credit of the United States, coupon or registered bonds, in sums not less than $50, to an amount not exceeding $500,000,000, redeemable at the pleasure of the United States after five years, and payable twenty years from date, and bearing interest at the rate of six per cent. per annum, payable semi-annually.

Over-subscription and further authorization.

Subscription books were opened to the public for this loan, and upon closing the same, at the time specified in the advertisement, it was found that $511,000,000 had been subscribed for. Congress, by act of March 3, 1864, chapter 17, section 2, authorized the issue of that amount, and by act of January 28, 1865, chapter 22, as construed, increased the amount authorized $4,000,000 more, making in all $515,000,000.

There were actually issued $439,422,000 coupon, and $75,349,600 registered bonds.

Title and designation.

The title was derived from the time after which the bonds might be redeemed—five years; the time when payable—

twenty years; and the year of the passage of the first act of authorization—1862.

The bonds bear on their face the designation, "REDEEMABLE AFTER FIVE AND PAYABLE TWENTY YEARS FROM DATE," and "LOAN OF FEBRUARY 25, 1862;" and are made redeemable at the pleasure of the United States after the 30th day of April, 1867, and payable on the first day of May, 1882, (except the first series, as hereafter explained,) with interest at six per cent. per annum, payable on the first days of May and November in each year.

Interest.

Series.

First.

The coupon bonds were issued in four series. Those of the first, amounting to one hundred millions of dollars, are printed in green tint, and have no designation of series upon them. They are made payable *after*, instead of *on*, the 1st day of May, 1882. This was an error in not following the language of the law, and was corrected in the subsequent series.

Second.

Those of the second, also of one hundred millions of dollars, are printed in yellow tint, with blue numbering, and have the words "SECOND SERIES," or "2D SERIES," stamped upon them, twice on the bond and once on each coupon.

Third.

Those of the third, also of one hundred millions of dollars, are printed in black, with blue numbering, and have "THIRD SERIES" stamped twice on the bonds and once on each coupon.

Fourth.

Those of the fourth, amounting to $139,422,000, are printed in black, with red numbering, and stamped as "FOURTH SERIES," or "4TH," in different styles and forms.

Denomination.

The bonds are $50, $100, $500, and $1,000 coupon and registered, and also $5,000 and $10,000 registered.

Redemption.

Section 4 of the refunding act of July 14, 1870, (chapter 256,) authorizes the Secretary of the Treasury to pay at par and cancel any five-twenty bonds after becoming redeemable, indicating and specifying, in public notices, by class, date, and number, in the order of their numbers and issues, beginning with the first numbered and issued, and declares that, in three months after the date of such public notice, the interest on the bonds, so selected and advertised to be paid, should cease. By virtue of this law the Secretary has called in for payment the following designated bonds, and has given notice thereof: Bonds called in for payment.

FIRST CALL.—*Notice dated September* 1, 1871. First call.

All the first series of coupon bonds of—

| | | |
|---|---|---|
| $50 | numbered | 1 to 30,699 inclusive. |
| $100 | " | 1 to 43,572 " |
| $500 | " | 1 to 40,011 " |
| $1,000 | " | 1 to 74,104 " |

All registered bonds of—

| | | |
|---|---|---|
| $50 | numbered | 1 to 595 inclusive. |
| $100 | " | 1 to 4,103 " |
| $500 | " | 1 to 1,899 " |
| $1,000 | " | 1 to 8,906 " |
| $5,000 | " | 1 to 2,665 " |
| $10,000 | " | 1 to 2,906 " |

Which ceased to bear interest December 1, 1871.

SECOND CALL.—*Notice dated December* 7, 1871. Second call.

Of the second series, all coupon bonds of—

| | | |
|---|---|---|
| $50 | numbered | 1 to 5,460 inclusive. |
| $100 | " | 1 to 13,093 " |
| $500 | " | 1 to 7,964 " |
| $1,000 | " | 1 to 11,120 " |

All registered bonds of—

| | | |
|---|---|---|
| $50 | numbered | 596 to 697 inclusive. |
| $100 | " | 4,104 to 5,079 " |
| $500 | " | 1,900 to 2,483 " |
| $1,000 | " | 8,907 to 11,008 " |
| $5,000 | " | 2,666 to 3,402 " |
| $10,000 | " | 2,907 to 3,899 " |

Which ceased to bear interest March 7, 1872.

THIRD CALL.—*Notice dated December* 20, 1871. Third call.

Of the second series, all coupon bonds of—

| | | |
|---|---|---|
| $50 | numbered | 5,461 to 10,775 inclusive. |
| $100 | " | 13,094 to 25,935 " |
| $500 | " | 7,965 to 16,179 " |
| $1,000 | " | 11,121 to 27,443 " |

All registered bonds of—

| | | |
|---|---|---|
| $50 | numbered | 698 to 840 inclusive. |
| $100 | " | 5,080 to 5,991 " |
| $500 | " | 2,484 to 2,958 " |
| $1,000 | " | 11,009 to 13,150 " |
| $5,000 | " | 3,403 to 4,102 " |
| $10,000 | " | 3,900 to 4,774 " |

Which ceased to bear interest March 20, 1872.

FOURTH CALL.—*Notice dated March* 1, 1873. Fourth call.

Of the second series, all coupon bonds of—

| | | |
|---|---|---|
| $50 | numbered | 10,776 to 27,798 inclusive. |
| $100 | " | 25,936 to 66,646 " |
| $500 | " | 16,180 to 41,373 " |
| $1,000 | " | 27,444 to 71,259 " |

Fourth call.

Of the third series, all coupon bonds of—

| | | | |
|---|---|---|---|
| $50 | numbered | 1 to | 1,200 inclusive. |
| $100 | " | 1 to | 4,752 " |
| $500 | " | 1 to | 3,000 " |
| $1,000 | " | 1 to | 5,733 " |

All registered bonds of—

| | | | |
|---|---|---|---|
| $50 | numbered | 841 to | 1,233 inclusive. |
| $100 | " | 5,992 to | 8,803 " |
| $500 | " | 2,959 to | 5,360 " |
| $1,000 | " | 13,151 to | 20,680 " |
| $5,000 | " | 4,103 to | 6,402 " |
| $10,000 | " | 4,775 to | 7,092 " |

Which cease to bear interest June 1, 1873.

Amount paid.

Besides the bonds thus called in for redemption, amounting to about $190,000,000, much of this loan has been purchased at the monthly purchases in New York.

Regulations for paying called bonds and coupons.

For regulations of the Treasury Department as to paying bonds called in for redemption, when coupons have been detached therefrom, and the payment of coupons thus detached, *see Chapter V, p.* 75.

11.

## LOAN OF JULY AND AUGUST, 1861;

or

## SIXES OF 1881.

Acts of authorization.

By the act of July 17, 1861, chapter 5, the Secretary of the Treasury was authorized to borrow on the credit of the United States a sum not exceeding $250,000,000, and to issue bonds therefor, or treasury notes, in such proportions as he might deem advisable, the bonds to bear interest not exceeding six per cent. per annum, payable semi-annually, irredeemable for twenty years, and after that period redeemable at the pleasure of the United States.

This law was amended by a supplementary act of August 5, 1861, chapter 46, of which section 1 authorized the Secretary to issue bonds bearing interest at six per cent. per annum, and payable at the pleasure of the United States after twenty years from date, but no such bond to be issued for a less sum than five hundred dollars, and to exchange the same for treasury notes issued under the former act. Section 7 of the act of August 5 also provided, that the Secretary might sell or negotiate, for any portion of the loan provided for by the act of July 17, bonds payable not more than twenty years from date, and bearing interest not exceeding six per cent. per annum, payable semi-annually.

There was issued under these various provisions one loan, by sale $50,000,000, and by exchange $139,321,200, in bonds redeemable after the 30th day of June, 1881, with interest at six per cent. per annum, payable on the 1st days of January and July in each year, designated on the face of each bond, "LOAN OF JULY 17, AND AUGUST 5, 1861," from which the official title of the loan was derived. The bonds are also called in the market, "SIXES OF 1881," from the rate of interest and time of payment.

Bonds issued. Interest. Payable. Designation and title.

The denominations actually issued are $50, $100, $500, and $1,000 coupon and registered bonds, and also $5,000 and $10,000 registered. The whole amount of the original loan is still outstanding, not having yet matured.

Denomination. Not matured.

## 12.

## OREGON WAR DEBT.

The act of March 2, 1861, chapter 70, entitled "An act to provide for the payment of expenses incurred by the Territories of Washington and Oregon in the suppression of Indian hostilities therein, in the years 1855 and 1856," appropriated so much money as might be necessary for the payment of specific claims therein mentioned, and by section 4 authorized the Secretary of the Treasury, if he deemed it expedient, to issue to the claimants bonds of the United States of a denomination not less than fifty dollars, redeemable in twenty years, and bearing interest at the rate of six per cent. per annum, with coupons attached, and payable annually or semi-annually, at the discretion of the Secretary.

Act of authorization.

Under this act there were issued $1,090,850, all in coupon bonds, payable at any time after the first day of July, 1881, to a payee therein named, *or order*, in denominations of $50 and $100, with interest at six per cent., payable annually, July 1, in each year, and of $500, with interest

Bonds issued. Denominations. Interest.

at the same rate, payable semi-annually, January 1 and July 1.

Title and designation.

The bonds are designated on the face, "OREGON WAR DEBT," and the loan takes its title from that fact.

Bonds payable to order.

These bonds, unlike any other coupon bonds, being payable to order, do not pass by delivery, but only by assignments, duly executed in like manner as those required on registered bonds, by the payee or assignee thereof.

Coupons.

The coupons pass by delivery.

Of this loan $145,850 have been redeemed, and the balance, $945,000, will become redeemable July 1, 1881.

## 13.

## LOAN OF FEBRUARY, 1861;

or

## SIXES OF 1881.

Act of authorization.

By the act of February 8, 1861, chapter 29, the President was authorized, at any time before the 1st day of July then next, to borrow, on the credit of the United States, a sum not exceeding twenty-five millions of dollars, to be used in the payment of the current demands upon the Treasury, and for the redemption of treasury notes outstanding, and to issue registered or coupon certificates of stock therefor, in sums not less than one thousand dollars, to be reimbursed within a period not beyond twenty years, and not less than ten years, with interest not exceeding six per cent. per annum, payable annually or semi-annually.

Bonds issued.

There were issued $18,415,000, in coupon bonds of $1,000, and registered bonds of $1,000, $5,000, and $10,000, redeemable AFTER, or at *any time after*, the 31st day of December,

Interest.

1880, with interest at six per cent. per annum, payable semi-annually, January 1 and July 1, in each year.

Payable.

The whole amount is still outstanding, and, notwithstanding the language of the bonds, is payable December 31, 1880—the extreme limit of time allowed by the act.

Title.

The title of the loan on the books of the Department is taken from the act of authorization, but the bonds are called in the market "SIXES OF 1881," on account of the time when they are supposed to become payable—January 1, 1881. These differ from the other Sixes of 1881, which are redeemable *after* June 30, 1881; while these are payable December 31, 1880.

## 14.

## LOAN OF 1858; or FIVES OF 1874.

Acts of authorization.

Tho President was authorized by act of Congress approved June 14, 1858, chapter 165, at any time within twelve months thereafter, to borrow, on the credit of the United States, a sum not exceeding twenty millions of dollars, provided no contract was to be made to prevent the United States from reimbursing the same at any time after fifteen years from the 1st day of January then next The stock was required to be issued in certificates of not less than $1,000 each, bearing interest not exceeding five per centum per annum, payable semi-annually, with interest coupons attached. By section 6 of the act of March 3, 1859, chapter 82, the Secretary of the Treasury was authorized to issue coupon or registered stock, as the purchaser might elect.

Title and designation of bonds.

The loan takes its title from the year of the passage of the act, and the bonds are designated on the face thereof with the words "UNITED STATES LOAN OF 1858." They are known in the market also under the name of "FIVES OF 1874," from the rate of interest and the time when they are supposed to become payable.

Amount issued.

Twenty millions of dollars of bonds were issued in denominations of $1,000, with coupons attached, and $1,000 and $5,000 registered.

Coupon bonds.

The language of the coupon bonds is that the "United States will pay unto —— or ——, the sum of ——, *at any time after* the 1st day of January, 1874." * * "Interest will be paid thereon at the rate of five per cent. per annum from the 1st day of January, 1859, payable semi-annually, on the 1st day of January and July of each year." * *

Registered.

That of the registered stock is "the principal of which is redeemable at the pleasure of the United States at any time after the expiration of fifteen years after the 1st of January, 1859, and bearing interest at the rate of five per cent. per annum, payable half yearly." The times of payment of interest are not specified in the registered stock, but are, in fact, the same as on the coupon bonds—January 1 and July 1 in each year.

Interest.

The oldest loan.

The whole loan is outstanding, not having yet matured, and is the oldest of all the outstanding loans of the United States not called in for redemption.

# CHAPTER II.

DEBT WHICH HAS CEASED TO BEAR INTEREST, COIN CERTIFICATES, CERTIFICATES OF DEPOSIT, AND DEBT BEARING INTEREST IN CURRENCY.

1. Debt which has ceased to bear interest.
2. Coin certificates, or gold certificates.
3. Certificates of deposit.
4. Three per cent. certificates.
5. Navy pension fund.
6. Certificates of indebtedness of 1870.
7. Currency sixes, or Pacific Railway bonds.

## 1.

### DEBT WHICH HAS CEASED TO BEAR INTEREST.

Holders of Government securities are slow to send them in for redemption at maturity, even after interest has ceased to run upon them, and balances of loans remain many years uncalled for. **Balances of old loans.**

Of the numerous debts matured prior to the year 1837 there are still outstanding and unclaimed of the principal $57,665; and of all loans heretofore matured the amount which had not been presented for payment September 1, 1872, was $6,170,675 26.

It is probable that some part of the bonds and other evidences of these outstanding balances have been destroyed by fire, shipwreck, and otherwise; and by reason of the death of the owners, or other causes, all knowledge of the existence of the indebtedness has passed away from those who might be entitled to avail themselves of the claims.

The Government sets up no statute of limitations against matured bonds, and pays those which have been destroyed, upon proof of destruction and ownership, at any period of time. **No statute of limitation.**

Of all the bonds matured and all issues of notes and currency called in for redemption, I am assured by those who have carefully examined the books of the Treasury Depart- **No over-issues.**

ment from its foundation, that in no case has there been redeemed or presented for payment any more than the books of the Government show to have been properly issued; and it is to the credit of the Treasury Department, and exhibits in a most striking manner the perfection of its organization as well as the honesty, integrity, and accuracy of its officers and employés, under all administrations for a period of over seventy-five years, that, in issuing more than seven billions of dollars in securities of all kinds, including bonds, certificates, and notes, there has never been a dollar of fraudulent over-issue.

## 2.

## COIN CERTIFICATES, OR GOLD CERTIFICATES

Are authorized by the following section of the act of the 3d of March, 1863, chapter 73:

SEC. 5. *And be it further enacted,* That the Secretary of the Treasury is hereby authorized to receive deposits of gold coin and bullion with the Treasurer or any Assistant Treasurer of the United States, in sums not less than twenty dollars, and to issue certificates therefor, in denominations of not less than twenty dollars each, corresponding with the denominations of the United States notes. The coin and bullion deposited for or representing the certificates of deposit shall be retained in the Treasury for the payment of the same on demand.

And certificates representing coin in the Treasury may be issued in payment of interest on the public debt, which certificates, together with those issued for coin and bullion deposited, shall not at any time exceed twenty per centum beyond the amount of coin and bullion in the Treasury; and the certificates for coin or bullion in the Treasury shall be received at par in payment for duties on imports.

Designations, denominations, &c. These certificates are now designated on the face thereof by the words "SERIES OF 1871," "ACT OF MARCH 3, 1863," and "GOLD CERTIFICATES;" are in denominations of $100, $500, $1,000, $5,000, and $10,000, payable at the office of the Assistant Treasurer at New York, where they are dated and countersigned by him, and are made payable to the order of a payee therein named. Where issued, &c. They are all issued from the Treasury at Washington through the Assistant Treasurer at New York, who, upon requisition, supplies them to other Assistant Treasurers and to Designated Depositaries, to be paid out to parties desiring them in settlement of interest on the public debt. By the present rules of the Department they are exchangeable for coin, and redeemed in coin only by the Assistant Treasurers at New York and Boston. They are receivable for duties everywhere.

Other series have been issued; some of those of 1870 were designated "GOLD NOTES," and an earlier series still had the denomination of $20; but as these certificates are never reissued when once redeemed by the Treasurer at Washington, all except those of the series of 1871 will soon disappear from circulation. Old series.

When indorsed in blank these certificates pass by delivery, and to some extent form a circulating medium of gold notes, especially in New York city, where the large gold transactions in the payment of duties and other business render them of great convenience.

The amount that may be issued is limited only by the wants and ability of the business community and the requirement of law that they shall not at any time exceed twenty per cent. beyond the amount of coin and bullion in the Treasury. Limit of issues.

### 3.

### CERTIFICATES OF DEPOSIT

Are issued according to the provisions of the following act of Congress, of June 8, 1872, chapter 346:

AN ACT FOR THE BETTER SECURITY OF BANK RESERVES, AND TO FACILITATE BANK CLEARING-HOUSE EXCHANGES.

*Be it enacted by the Senate and House of Representatives of the United States of America in Congress assembled*, That the Secretary of the Treasury is hereby authorized to receive United States notes on deposit, without interest, from national banking associations, in sums not less than ten thousand dollars, and to issue certificates therefor in such form as the Secretary may prescribe, in denominations of not less than five thousand dollars; which certificate shall be pay- Law of authorization.

able on demand in United States notes at the place where the deposits were made.

SEC. 2. That the United States notes so deposited in the Treasury of the United States shall not be counted as part of the legal reserve; but the certificates issued therefor may be held and counted by national banks as part of their legal reserve, and may be accepted in the settlement of clearing-house balances at the places where the deposits therefor were made.

SEC. 3. That nothing contained in this act shall be construed to authorize any expansion or contraction of the currency; and the United States notes for which such certificates are issued, or other United States notes of like amount, shall be held as special deposits in the Treasury, and used only for the redemption of such certificates.

*Approved June* 8, 1872.

Designation, &c.

The certificates are designated on the face thereof with the words "CERTIFICATE OF DEPOSIT," "UNITED STATES NOTES," and "ACT OF JUNE 8, 1872, chapter 346," are in denominations of $5,000 and $10,000, are signed by the Treasurer and Register of the Treasury and countersigned by the Assistant Treasurer by whom they are issued, and are made payable to the order of a payee therein named, in United States notes, on demand, at the office of the Assistant Treasurer where they are countersigned and dated.

## 4.

## THREE PER CENT. CERTIFICATES;

or

## TEMPORARY LOAN CERTIFICATES.

Law of authorization.

The act of March 2, 1867, (chapter 194,) for the purpose of redeeming and retiring any compound-interest notes outstanding, directed the Secretary of the Treasury to issue temporary loan certificates, bearing interest at a rate not exceeding three per cent. per annum; the principal and interest payable in lawful money on demand, and provided that they might be held by any national bank as a part of its reserve required by law, to the extent of three-fifths of such reserve. The amount to be issued was by that act limited to fifty millions of dollars, and was extended to seventy-five millions of dollars by the act of July 25, 1868. The whole amount actually issued has been about eighty-four millions of dollars, but not over seventy-five millions at any one time. They are all, or nearly all, held by the banks, and the interest has been paid upon them semi-annually.

From the commencement of issuing these certificates in payment of compound-interest notes they have been canceled as fast as redeemed by the Treasury Department, and never reissued. The amount outstanding was gradually reduced, by being presented for payment from time to time, whenever legal-tender notes were needed by the holders, until it was less than forty-six millions of dollars on the 12th of July, 1870. At that date Congress passed an act authorizing the increase of national bank circulation to the extent of fifty-four millions of dollars, and requiring the redemption of these certificates monthly to the amount of the issue of new bank circulation during the preceding months, as reported to the Secretary by the Comptroller of the Currency. Under the operation of this requirement the three per cent. certificates are being called in for payment, and will soon disappear from the reports of the outstanding debt, except such as may remain unclaimed after interest thereon has ceased to run. Gradual redemption.

## 5.

## NAVY PENSION FUND.

This fund arises from the money accruing to the United States from the capture of prizes authorized by law, and is set apart for the payment of pensions to the officers, seamen, and marines who may be entitled to receive the same, and if the fund is insufficient for that purpose, the public faith is pledged to make up the deficiency. Origin and object of the fund.

It is established and managed under the following laws: Act of April 23, 1800, chapter 33, sections 9 and 10, (a substitute for act of March 2, 1799, chapter 24;) act of March 26, 1804, chapter 48; act of April 16, 1816, chapter 56;

resolution of July 1, 1864, chapter 62; act of July 23, 1868, chapter 229, section 2; and act of July 20, 1868; and there are many acts authorizing payment therefrom.

The fund amounts to fourteen millions of dollars, for which no bonds have been issued, and of which no evidence of indebtedness exists, except what appears in the laws of Congress and the books of the Treasury Department.

It would hardly be called a debt, were it not included in the monthly debt statement of the Department; and since the passage of the act of July 23, 1868, providing that the interest on the fund shall be at the rate of three per cent. per annum, in lawful money, and applicable exclusively to the payment of navy pensions, it amounts simply to a permanent appropriation of four hundred and twenty thousand dollars a year to the payment of navy pensions.

## 6.

## CERTIFICATES OF INDEBTEDNESS OF 1870.

Law authorizing issue.

The act of July 8, 1870, chapter 229, authorized the issue of certificates of indebtedness of the denomination of $1,000 each, to the amount of $678,362 41, payable in lawful money of the United States in five years, with interest semi-annually at the rate of four per cent. per annum, two-thirds to the State of Massachusetts, and one-third to the State of Maine, for the use of the European and North American Railway Company of Maine, to aid said company in constructing its line of railway; each of said States having assigned its interest therein to said railway company. These bonds were, by the act, to be in "full adjustment and payment for and on account of any matters arising from any money expended by said State of Massachusetts on account of the war with Great Britain in 1812 to 1815, or any interest thereon, or on account of any matters arising out of or accruing from the treaty with Great Britain, known as the treaty of Washington, or for or on account of any other matters which have been assigned by said States of Massachusetts and Maine to said railway company."

Amount issued.

There were issued 678 certificates of $1,000 each, payable to the Treasurer of the State of Maine or bearer, in five years from September 1, 1870, with semi-annual interest coupons of twenty dollars each attached, both payable in lawful money. The coupons are payable March 1 and September 1. These certificates are all outstanding, and will become payable September 1, 1875. For the balance, $362 11, one other certificate was issued, and has since been paid and canceled.

—when payable, &c.

## 7.

## CURRENCY SIXES;

## or

## PACIFIC RAILWAY BONDS.

Title, denominations, designations, &c.

These bonds are commonly known as "CURRENCY SIXES," because they bear six per cent. interest, and are the only bonds of the United States payable, principal and interest, in lawful money. On the public debt statement and the books of the Treasury Department they are called "PACIFIC RAILWAY BONDS," on account of their having been issued to certain Pacific railroads in the nature of a loan, under acts of Congress to aid in the construction of their roads.

They are all registered, in denominations of $1,000, $5,000, and $10,000; are payable in lawful money on a day therein named, which is at the expiration of thirty years from the date of original issue, with interest at six per cent. per annum, payable semi-annually, on the 1st days of January and July in each year, in lawful money; and are designated with the words "[NAME OF COMPANY] RAILROAD COMPANY," "PAYABLE THIRTY YEARS FROM DATE," and "Act of July 1st, 1862, Act of July 2d, 1864."

The name of a railroad company is thus printed on the bonds merely to indicate to which company they were issued.

United States alone responsible to holder.

They are the bonds of the United States, containing the absolute unconditional promise of the national Government, and the Government alone is responsible for the payment of both principal and interest. The railroad companies are under no obligations to the holders of the bonds, but only to repay the United States, in the manner set forth in the acts of Congress.

Bonds issued.

THE FOLLOWING TABLE EXHIBITS THE NAMES OF THE COMPANIES TO WHICH THE BONDS WERE ISSUED, THE AMOUNT, DATE OF ISSUE, AND TIMES OF BECOMING PAYABLE.

| Names of companies to which the bonds were issued. | Amount issued. | Date of issue. | Payable. |
|---|---|---|---|
| Central Pacific.................. | $2,362,000 | Jan'y 16, 1865. | Jan'y 16, 1895. |
| " " .................... | 1,600,000 | Jan'y 1, 1866. | Jan'y 1, 1896. |
| " " .................... | 2,112,000 | Jan'y 1, 1867. | Jan'y 1, 1897. |
| " " .................... | 10,614,120 | Jan'y 1, 1868. | Jan'y 1, 1898. |
| " " .................... | 9,197,000 | Jan'y 1, 1869. | Jan'y 1, 1899. |
| Union Pacific..................... | 4,320,000 | Feb'y 1, 1866. | Feb'y 1, 1896. |
| " " .................... | 3,840,000 | Jan'y 1, 1867. | Jan'y 1, 1897. |
| " " .................... | 15,919,512 | Jan'y 1, 1868. | Jan'y 1, 1898. |
| " " .................... | 3,157,000 | Jan'y 1, 1869. | Jan'y 1, 1899. |
| Central Branch Union Pacific, late Atchison and Pike's Peak.............................. | 640,000 | Jan'y 1, 1866. | Jan'y 1, 1896. |
| " " .................... | 640,000 | Jan'y 1, 1867. | Jan'y 1, 1897. |
| " " .................... | 320,000 | Jan'y 1, 1868. | Jan'y 1, 1898. |
| Kansas, late Union Pacific, Eastern Division............. | 640,000 | Nov'r 1, 1865. | Nov'r 1, 1895. |
| " " ...... ............ | 1,440,000 | Jan'y 1, 1866. | Jan'y 1, 1896. |
| " " .................... | 2,800,000 | Jan'y 1, 1867. | Jan'y 1, 1897. |
| " " .................... | 1,423,000 | Jan'y 1, 1868. | Jan'y 1, 1898. |
| Western Pacific.................. | 320,000 | Jan'y 1, 1867. | Jan'y 1, 1897. |
| " " .................... | 1,650,560 | Jan'y 1, 1869 | Jan'y 1, 1899. |
| Sioux City and Pacific.......... | 1,628,320 | Jan'y. 1, 1868 | Jan'y 1, 1898. |

Interest payable January 1 and July 1.

These bonds were issued under the act of July 1, 1862, chapter 120, and the act of July 2, 1864, chapter 216, as amended by some subsequent provisions.

Grants by United States.

A right of way and certain public lands were thereby granted to the railroad companies, and provisions made requiring the Secretary of the Treasury to issue the bonds above mentioned to said companies, upon completing sections of their road, at the rate of sixteen thousand dollars per mile, except for certain parts more difficult of construction, for which they were to be issued at the rate respectively of thirty-two thousand and forty-eight thousand dollars per mile. The security of the United States rests upon the following provisions of law:

Security for repayment of bonds.

ACT OF JULY 2, 1862, CHAPTER 120.

SEC. 5. * * * and to secure the repayment to the United States, as hereinafter provided, of the amount of said bonds so issued and delivered to said company, together with all interest thereon which shall have been paid by the United States, the issue of said bonds and delivery to the company shall *ipso facto* constitute *a first* mortgage on the whole line of the railroad and telegraph, together with the rolling stock, fixtures, and property of every kind and description, and in consideration of which said bonds may be issued;

Mortgage.

And on the refusal or failure of the said company to redeem said bonds, or any part of them, when required so to do by the Secretary of the Treasury, in accordance with the provisions of this act, the said road, with all the rights, functions, immunities, and appurtenances thereunto belonging, and also all lands granted to the said company by the United States, which, at the time of said default, shall remain in the ownership of said company, may be taken possession of by the Secretary of the Treasury, for the use and benefit of the United States: *Provided*, This section shall not apply to that part of any road now constructed.

Road, &c., to be forfeited on failure of company to redeem bonds

SEC. 6. *And be it further enacted*, That the grants aforesaid are made upon condition, that said company shall pay said bonds at maturity, and shall keep said railroad and telegraph line in repair and use, and shall at all times transmit dispatches over said telegraph line, and transport mails, troops, and munitions of war, supplies, and public stores upon said railroad for the Government, whenever required to do so by any department thereof, and that the Government shall at all times have the preference in the use of the same for all the purposes aforesaid, (at fair and reasonable rates of compensation, not to exceed the amounts paid by private parties for the same kind of service;)

Grants on condition that companies shall pay bonds at maturity.

And all compensation for services rendered for the Government shall be applied to the payment of said bonds and interest until the whole amount is fully paid. Said company may also pay the United States, wholly or in part, in the same or other bonds, treasury notes, or other evidences of debt against the United States, to be allowed at par;

Compensation for services to U. S. to be retained. Companies may pay in treasury notes, bonds, &c.

And after said road is completed, until said bonds and interest are paid, at least five per centum of the net earnings of said road shall also be annually applied to the payment thereof.

—after completion of roads 5 per cent. of net earnings to be applied to payment of bonds.

The lien of the United States is made subordinate to a

Government lien.

and mortgage to be second and subordinate to a prior mortgage of same amount.

first mortgage authorized by the provisions of the act of July 2, 1864, chapter 216, as follows:

SEC. 10. *And be it further enacted*, That section five of said act be so modified and amended, that the Union Pacific Railroad Company, the Central Pacific Railroad Company, and any other company authorized to participate in the construction of said road, may, on the completion of each section of said road, as provided in this act and the act of which this is an amendment, issue their first mortgage bonds on their respective railroads and telegraph lines, to an amount not exceeding the amount of the bonds of the United States, and of even tenor and date, time of maturity, rate and character of interest with the bonds authorized to be issued to said railroads respectively.

And the lien of the United States bonds shall be subordinate to that of the bonds of any or either of said companies hereby authorized to be issued on their respective roads, property, and equipments, except as to the provisions of the sixth section of the act to which this act is an amendment, relating to the transmission of dispatches and the transportation of mails, troops, munitions of war, supplies, and public stores for the Government of the United States.

Section 5, chapter 216, act of July 2, 1864, provides—

Only half of compensation for services to U. S. to be retained.

That only *one half* of the compensation for services rendered for the Government by said companies shall be required to be applied to the payment of the bonds issued by the Government in aid of the construction of said road.

And the act of March 3, 1871, chapter 116—

Balance to be paid to companies.

SEC. 9. That, in accordance with the fifth section of the act approved July two, eighteen hundred and sixty-four, entitled "An act to amend an act entitled 'An act to aid in the construction of a railroad and telegraph line from the Missouri river to the Pacific ocean, and to secure to the Government the use of the same for postal, military, and other purposes,' approved July first, eighteen hundred and sixty-two," the Secretary of the Treasury is hereby directed to pay over in money to the Pacific Railroad Companies mentioned in said act, and performing services for the United States, one-half of the compensation at the rate provided by law for such services, heretofore or hereafter rendered: *Provided*, That this section shall not be construed to affect the legal rights of the Government or the obligations of the companies, except as herein specifically provided.

# CHAPTER III.

## UNITED STATES NOTES AND FRACTIONAL CURRENCY; DISTINCTIVE PAPER; EXCHANGE OF MUTILATED AND DEFACED NOTES, ETC.



1.

### UNITED STATES NOTES,

Commonly called "LEGAL-TENDER NOTES," from being made by law a legal tender for debts; and "GREENBACKS," from the green color in which the backs have always been printed. They are issued under the following provisions of law:

ACT OF FEBRUARY 25, 1862, CHAPTR 33, SECTION 1.

*Be it enacted by the Senate and House of Representatives of the United States of America in Congress assembled,* Acts of authorization. First act.

That the Secretary of the Treasury is hereby authorized to issue, on the credit of the United States, one hundred and fifty millions of dollars of United States notes, not bearing interest, payable to bearer, at the Treasury of the United States and of such denominations as he may deem expedient, not less than five dollars each:

*Provided, however*, That fifty millions of said notes shall be in lieu of the demand treasury notes authorized to be issued by the act of July seventeen, eighteen hundred and sixty-one; which said demand notes shall be taken up as rapidly as practicable, and the notes herein provided for substituted for them: *And provided further*, That the amount of the two kinds of notes together shall at no time exceed the sum of one hundred and fifty millions of dollars;

And such notes herein authorized shall be receivable in payment of all taxes, internal duties, excises, debts, and demands of every kind due to the United States, except duties on imports, and of all claims and demands against the United States of every kind whatsoever, except for interest upon bonds and notes, which shall be paid in coin, and shall also be lawful money and a legal tender in payment of all debts, public and private, within the United States, except duties on imports and interest as aforesaid. And any holders of said United States notes, depositing any sum not less than fifty dollars or some multiple of fifty dollars, with the Treasurer of the United States, or either of the Assistant Treasurers, shall receive in exchange therefor duplicate certificates of deposit, one of which may be transmitted to the Secretary of the Treasury, who shall thereupon issue to the holder an equal amount of bonds of the United States, coupon or registered, as may by said holder be desired, bearing interest at the rate of six per centum per annum, payable semi-annually, and redeemable at the pleasure of the United States after five years, and payable twenty years from the date thereof.

And such United States notes shall be received the same as coin, at their par value, in payment for any loans that may be hereafter sold or negotiated by the Secretary of the Treasury, and may be reissued from time to time, as the exigencies of the public interest shall require.

* * * * * * *

ACT OF JULY 11, 1862, CHAPTER 142.

Second act. *Be it enacted by the Senate and House of Representatives of the United States of America in Congress assembled,*

That the Secretary of the Treasury is hereby authorized to issue, in addition to the amounts heretofore authorized, on the credit of the United States, one hundred and fifty millions of dollars of United States notes, not bearing interest, payable to bearer, at the Treasury of the United States, and of such denominations as he may deem expedient:

*Provided*, That no note shall be issued for the fractional part of a dollar, and not more than thirty-five millions shall be of lower denominations than five dollars.

And such notes shall be receivable in payment of all loans made to the United States, and of all taxes, internal duties, excises, debts, and demands of every kind due to the United States, except duties on imports and interest, and of all claims and demands against the United States, except for interest upon bonds, notes, and certificates of debt or deposit; and shall also be lawful money and a legal tender in payment of all debts, public and private, within the United States, except duties on imports and interest, as aforesaid.

And any holder of said United States notes, depositing any sum not less than fifty dollars, or some multiple of fifty dollars, with the Treasurer of the United States, or either of the Assistant Treasurers, shall receive in exchange therefor duplicate certificates of deposit, one of which may be transmitted to the Secretary of the Treasury, who shall thereupon issue to the holder an equal amount of bonds of the United States, coupon or registered, as may by said holder be desired, bearing interest at the rate of six per centum per annum, payable semi-annually, and redeemable at the pleasure of the United States after five years, and payable twenty years from the date thereof:

*Provided, however,* That any notes issued under this act may be paid in coin, instead of being received in exchange for certificates of deposit as above specified, at the direction of the Secretary of the Treasury.

And the Secretary of the Treasury may exchange for such notes, on such terms as he shall think most beneficial to the public interest, any bonds of the United States bearing six per centum interest, and redeemable after five and payable in twenty years, which have been or may be lawfully issued under the provisions of any existing act;

May reissue the notes so received in exchange; may receive and cancel any notes heretofore lawfully issued under any act of Congress, and in lieu thereof issue an equal amount in notes such as are authorized by this act;

* * * * * * *

SEC. 3. * * * * * *

And of the amounts of United States notes authorized by this act, not less than fifty millions of dollars shall be reserved for the purpose of securing prompt payment of such deposits, [*temporary loan deposits authorized by the same act,*] when demanded, and shall be issued and used only when, in the judgment of the Secretary of the Treasury, the same or any part thereof may be needed for that purpose. * *

ACT OF MARCH 3, 1863, CHAPTER 73.

* * * * * * *

SEC. 3. *And be it further enacted,* That the Secretary of the Treasury be, and he is hereby, authorized, if required by the exigencies of the public service, for the payment of the army and navy, and other creditors of the Government, to issue, on the credit of the United States, the sum of one hundred and fifty millions of dollars of United States notes, including the amount of such notes heretofore authorized by the joint resolution approved January seventeen, eighteen hundred and sixty-three, in such form as he may deem expedient, not bearing interest, payable to bearer, and of such denominations, not less than one dollar, as he may prescribe, Third act.

which notes so issued shall be lawful money and a legal tender in payment of all debts, public and private, within the United States, except for duties on imports and interest on the public debt; and any of the said notes, when returned to the Treasury, may be reissued from time to time as the exigencies of the public service may require.

And in lieu of any of said notes, or any other United States notes, returned to the Treasury and canceled or destroyed, there may be issued equal amounts of United States notes, such as are authorized by this act.

* * * * * * *

And the holders of United States notes, issued under and by virtue of said acts, [*of February* 25 *and July* 11, 1862,] shall present the same for the purpose of exchanging the same for bonds, as therein provided, on or before the 1st day of July, eighteen hundred and sixty-three, and thereafter the right so to exchange the same shall cease and determine.

The joint resolution referred to in the above act only authorized the issue of one hundred millions of dollars of notes in advance of the passage of that act then pending before Congress.

Limit of issue.

These three acts together authorize the issue of four hundred and fifty millions of dollars; but the construction given by the Treasury Department is that the fifty millions required by the act of July 11, 1862, (see page 37,) to be reserved for the payment of temporary deposits and used only when, in the judgment of the Secretary, the same, or any part thereof, might be necessary for that purpose, were intended by Congress to be a temporary issue, and when once withdrawn, by the reduction of the whole to four hundred millions, not to be reissued. This construction is sustained by the Supreme Court in the case of "*The Banks* v. *The Supervisors*, (7 *Wallace*, 26.) The Chief Justice, who was Secretary of the Treasury at the time of the passage of the acts, therein says: "The act of February 25, 1862, provided for the issue of these notes to the amount of one hundred and fifty millions of dollars. The act of July 11, 1862, added another hundred and fifty millions of dollars to the circulation, reserving, however, fifty millions for the redemption of temporary loan, to be issued and used only when necessary for that purpose. Under the act of March

3, 1863, another issue of one hundred and fifty millions was authorized, making the whole amount authorized four hundred and fifty millions, and contemplating a permanent circulation, until resumption of payment in coin, of four hundred millions of dollars." The same view was again expressed by the Chief Justice, in *Veazie Bank* v. *Fenno*, (8 *Wallace*, 537.)

**Highest amount issued. Reduction, &c.**

The amount in actual circulation, including demand notes, reached its highest point about August 31, 1865, when it was $433,160,569. At the time of the proclamation of the President, April 2, 1866, declaring the rebellion ended in certain States therein named, it was $422,749,252. It was first reduced below four hundred millions of dollars September 1, 1866, near the time of the President's proclamation of August 20, 1866, declaring the insurrection at an end throughout the whole of the United States, when it was $399,603,592, and has never been so high since that date.

**Limiting reduction.**

Congress passed the act of April 12, 1866, (chapter 39,) providing "that of United States notes not more than ten millions of dollars may be retired and canceled within six months from the passage of this act, and thereafter not more than four millions of dollars in any one month," and the Secretary of the Treasury thereafter continued to reduce the amount in circulation.

**Suspending further reduction.**

Afterwards Congress passed the following act, which became a law without the approval of the President on the 4th of February, 1868:

AN ACT TO SUSPEND FURTHER REDUCTION OF THE CURRENCY.

*Be it enacted by the Senate and House of Representatives of the United States of America in Congress assembled*, That from and after the passage of this act, the authority of the Secretary of the Treasury to make any reduction of the currency, by retiring or canceling United States notes, shall be, and is hereby, suspended; but nothing herein contained shall prevent the cancellation and destruction of mutilated United States notes, and the replacing the same with notes of the same character and amount.

At this time the amount outstanding was three hundred

and fifty-six millions of dollars, and that is the limit below which the circulation of United States notes cannot be reduced without congressional enactment.

The reserve of forty-four millions of notes.

Between that amount and the four hundred millions authorized by law, the issue of the reserve of forty-four millions of dollars is left to the discretion of the Secretary of the Treasury, who has temporarily issued portions of it on the following and other occasions of pressing necessity:

During the month of September, 1869, about a million and a half of dollars of the three per cent. demand certificates came in suddenly for redemption, and were paid out of this reserve; but the amount so withdrawn was again restored thereto within two weeks;

In the great Chicago fire of 1871 about a million and a half of dollars in notes were burned and entirely destroyed in the office of the depositary at that place, and the Secretary increased the apparent circulation by that amount from the reserve, until, by the seventh section of the act of June 10, 1872, chapter 415, Congress authorized the accounting officers to allow a credit of the burned notes in the accounts of the depositary and in the books of the Department when the amount was restored to the reserve.

Redemption of notes in coin.

The obligation of the Government to finally redeem all these notes in coin is expressed in the following language of the Chief Justice of the Supreme Court, in the case of *The Bank* v. *The Supervisors*, (7 *Wallace*, 29,) already referred to:

"Under the exigencies of the times it seems to have been thought inexpedient to attempt any provision for the redemption of the United States notes in coin.

"The law, therefore, directed that they should be made payable to bearer at the Treasury of the United States, but did not provide for payment on demand. The period of payment was left to be determined by the public exigencies." * * "Every one of them expresses upon its face an engagement of the nation to pay the bearer a certain sum. The dollar note is an engagement to pay a dollar, and the dollar intended is the coined dollar of the United States; a certain quantity in weight and fineness of gold or silver, authenticated as such by the stamp of the Government. No other dollars had before been recognized by the legislation of the national Government as lawful money."

Until the year 1870 it was a mooted question whether the provisions of law making United States notes a legal tender for debts public and private were constitutional or not. Their constitutionality was sustained by the decisions of several State courts of different States; but, *as to debts contracted before the passage of the laws*, it was, in 1869, held otherwise by the Supreme Court of the United States, in *Hepburn* v. *Griswold*, (8 *Wallace*, 603.) At that time two vacancies existed on the bench of that court, and the decision was not regarded throughout the country as conclusive upon the point raised. The question was again, in 1870, brought before the full court, consisting of nine judges, in the two cases of *Knox* v. *Lee* and *Parker* v. *Davis*, (12 *Wallace*, 457,) heard together, was elaborately argued, and the constitutionality of the law fully sustained by a majority of the court—four judges dissenting. Constitutionality of legal-tender provisions.

Mr. Justice Strong, in delivering the opinion of the court, says: "It will be seen that we hold the acts of Congress constitutional as applied to contracts made either before or after their passage. In so holding, we overrule so much of what was decided in *Hepburn* v. *Griswold* as ruled the acts unwarranted by the constitution so far as they apply to contracts made before their enactment. That case was decided by a divided court, and by a court having a less number of judges than the law then in existence provided this court shall have. These cases have been heard before a full court, and they have received our most careful consideration." —finally settled.

It may therefore be considered as finally settled, by the authoritative decision of the court of last resort, the Supreme Court of the United States, that the legal-tender acts, as they are commonly called, making United States notes a legal tender for debts, public and private, are constitutional and valid.

As to what are "debts" within the meaning of the legal-tender acts, and what debts may or may not be discharged by a tender of United States notes, there has been some conflict of authorities in the different courts, the State courts For what debts United States notes are not legal tenders.

generally going further than the Supreme Court of the United States in sustaining the application of the law. The following principles may be taken as now well established:

United States notes are not a legal tender for *taxes* imposed under State authority, unless made so by the laws of the State, (*Lane* v. *Oregon*, 7 *Wallace*, 71;) nor in payment of a promissory note expressly payable by its terms in coin, (*Vilhac* v. *Biven*, 28 *Cal.*, 410;) nor in discharge of a bond to pay a certain sum in gold and silver coin, (*Bronson* v. *Rodes*, 7 *Wallace*, 229;) nor in payment of the annual rent reserved by a lease made in 1791 in the words, "Fifteen pounds current money of Maryland, payable in English golden guineas, weighing five pennyweights and six grains, at thirty-five shillings each, and other gold and silver at their present established weight and rate, according to act of Assembly," (*Butler* v. *Horwitz*, 7 *Wallace*, 258;) nor in discharge of any contract made payable in specie or in commodities or obligations of any kind, but only for debts which are payable in money generally, (*Trebilcock* v. *Wilson et ux.*, 12 *Wallace*, 687;) nor in satisfaction of an award against the United States, made payable in coin by the terms of the award, (*Tyers* v. *United States*, 5 *Court of Claims Reports*, 509.)

Different issues. Under the three acts authorizing the issue of legal-tender notes, four different issues have been made. The first two differed from each other only slightly in the style and language of the notes. Those of the first were dated March 10, 1862, and bore on the face the words, "Act of February 25th, 1862." Those of the second were dated August 1, 1862, and bore on the face the words, "Act of July 11, 1862;" of this issue there were notes of the denominations of one dollar and two dollars, which were prohibited by the first, but allowed by the second act.

Exchangeable for bonds. All these notes, of both issues, had printed upon the backs thereof the declaration contained in the laws authorizing them, that they were "exchangeable for United States six per cent. twenty-year bonds, redeemable at the pleasure of the United States after five years." This right to exchange notes for five-twenty bonds was, by the third section of the act of March 3, 1863, chapter 73, limited to July 1, 1863, after which it ceased and determined. (*See page* 38.)

The next issue was under the act of 1863. The notes were dated March 10, 1863, bore on the face thereof the words, "Act of March 3d, 1863," and on the back, like those of the former issues, the words, "This note is a legal tender for all debts public and private, except duties on imports and interest on the public debt," but omitted the declaration that they were exchangeable for five-twenty bonds. In other respects they did not much differ from the earlier printed notes. **Next issue.**

The latest issue is that of the series of 1869, now most in circulation. All others are being redeemed as rapidly as possible, and are never reissued when once paid into the Treasury. Each note of this series has upon its face the words, "March 3d, 1863," and, unlike those of any other issue, the words, "TREASURY NOTE," and, except the $1,000 note, "Series of 1869." They differ from the others also in general style, in the details of engraving, in the tinting, and otherwise, besides being printed on the distinctive paper designated by the Secretary of the Treasury, and made under the supervision of the Treasury Department. **Latest issue.**

## 2.

## OLD DEMAND NOTES.

The act of July 17, 1861, chapter 5, authorized the issue of treasury notes, of denominations less than $50 and not less than $10, not bearing interest, payable on demand by the Assistant Treasurers of the United States at Philadelphia, New York, and Boston, not exceeding fifty millions in all. By section six the authority to issue and reissue these notes was limited, to cease and determine December 31, 1862. The amount to be issued was increased to sixty millions of dollars by the act of February 12, 1862. The act of August 5, 1861, permitted notes to be in denominations not less than $5, added the assistant treasury at Saint Louis and the depository at Cincinnati as places of redemption, and provided that the notes should be "receivable in **Laws relating to.**

payment of all public dues." The act of March 17, 1862, chapte· 45, further provided, that in addition to being receivable in payment of duties on imports, they should be receivable, and should be lawful money and a legal tender, in like manner and for the same purposes and to the same extent, as the notes authorized by the act of February 25, 1862. Sixty millions of dollars of these notes were issued, but none have been reissued since December 31, 1862; and all that are received into the Treasury are canceled and destroyed. Less than a hundred thousand dollars remain outstanding, and these, or all that are in existence, will soon be redeemed.

Description of notes.

They were dated August 10, 1861, were made payable on demand by the Assistant Treasurer at New York, and were stamped on the face with the words, "ACT OF JULY 17th, 1861," and "RECEIVABLE IN PAYMENT OF ALL PUBLIC DUES." These are the notes referred to in the law establishing the sinking fund, act of February 25, 1862, chapter 33, section 5, as receivable in payment of duties on imports, and are the only notes issued during the Rebellion, or since its close, payable *on demand* and receivable for duties. They are treated as gold notes, and are redeemed in coin whenever presented for payment.

Payable on demand in gold.

## 3.

## FRACTIONAL CURRENCY.

Origin of fractional currency.

The suspension of specie payments by the banks in December, 1861, was followed by the withdrawal of specie, gold, silver, and even copper coinage, from circulation, and the difficulties of making payments of small sums became so great, that the people were driven to the necessity of using postage stamps, revenue stamps, and the checks and memoranda of individuals and corporations, issued for that purpose, as a circulating medium for small change.

Acts of authorization.

In order to afford relief to the public from this great inconvenience, Congress passed the following acts, which are still in force, and under which the fractional currency is now issued:

ACT OF JULY 17, 1862, CHAPTER 196.

AN ACT TO AUTHORIZE PAYMENTS IN STAMPS, AND TO PROHIBIT CIRCULATION OF NOTES OF LESS DENOMINATION THAN ONE DOLLAR.

*Be it enacted by the Senate and House of Representatives of the United States of America in Congress assembled,*

That the Secretary of the Treasury be, and he is hereby, directed to furnish to the Assistant Treasurers, and such designated depositaries of the United States as may be by him selected, in such sums as he may deem expedient, the postage and other stamps of the United States, to be exchanged by them, on application, for United States notes; and from and after the 1st day of August next such stamps shall be receivable in payment of all dues to the United States less than five dollars, and shall be received in exchange for United States notes when presented to any Assistant Treasurer or any designated depositary selected as aforesaid in sums not less than five dollars. First act.

SEC. 2. *And be it further enacted,*

That from and after the first day of August, eighteen hundred and sixty-two, no private corporation, banking association, firm, or individual shall make, issue, circulate, or pay any note, check, memorandum, token, or other obligation, for a less sum than one dollar, intended to circulate as money or to be received or used in lieu of lawful money of the United States; and every person so offending shall, on conviction thereof in any district or circuit court of the United States, be punished by fine not exceeding five hundred dollars, or by imprisonment not exceeding six months, or by both, at the option of the court. Penalty for circulating, &c., other fractional currency.

*Approved July* 17, 1862.

ACT OF MARCH 3, 1863, CHAPTER 73.

SEC. 4. *And be it further enacted,* That in lieu of postage and revenue stamps for fractional currency, and of fractional notes, commonly called postage currency, issued or to be issued, the Secretary of the Treasury may issue fractional notes of like amounts, in such form as he may deem expedient, and may provide for the engraving, preparation, and issue thereof in the Treasury Department building. And all such notes issued shall be exchangeable by the Assistant Treasurers and designated depositaries for United States notes, in sums not less than three dollars, and shall be receivable for postage and revenue stamps, and also in payment of any dues to the United States less than five dollars, except duties on imports, and shall be redeemed on presentation at the Treasury of the United States in such sums Second act and under such regulations as the Secretary of the Treasury shall prescribe: *Provided*, That the whole amount of fractional currency issued, including postage and revenue stamps issued as currency, shall not exceed fifty millions of dollars.

Limited to fifty millions dollars

ACT OF JUNE 30, 1864, CHAPTER 172.

Third act.

SEC. 5. *And be it further enacted*, That the Secretary of the Treasury may issue notes of the fractions of a dollar as now used for currency, in such form, with such inscriptions, and with such safeguards against counterfeiting, as he may judge best, and provide for the engraving and preparation, and for the issue of the same, as well as of all other notes and bonds and other obligations, and shall make such regulations for the redemption of said fractional notes and other notes when mutilated or defaced, and for the receipt of said fractional notes in payment of debts to the United States, except for customs, in such sums, not over five dollars, as may appear to him expedient; and it is hereby declared that all laws and parts of laws applicable to the fractional notes engraved and issued as herein authorized apply equally and with like force to all the fractional notes heretofore authorized, whether known as postage currency or otherwise, and to postage stamps issued as currency; but the whole amount of all descriptions of notes or stamps less than one dollar issued as currency shall not exceed fifty millions of dollars.

Whole amount not to exceed fifty millions of dollars.

Postage currency.

On the 21st of August, 1862, the Treasury Department began to issue the first notes of denominations less than $1, under the act of July 17 of that year. They bore upon the face thereof the words "POSTAGE CURRENCY," and "Receivable for postage stamps at any post office," with *fac similes* of the designs of postage stamps. The 5-cent note had the print of a five-cent postage stamp, and the 10-cent note a ten-cent postage stamp. The 25-cent note had five five-cent postage stamps, and the 50-cent note five ten-cent postage stamps. This currency was used during the most excited and disturbed times of the Rebellion, and much of it was undoubtedly destroyed in the hands of holders, and will never come in for redemption. None of it has been reissued for many years, and the Department has made great efforts to withdraw it from circulation; but there are more than four millions of dollars still outstanding—a much larger amount than of either of the next two issues.

Fractional currency.

Since the passage of the acts of March 3, 1863, and June 30, 1864, several other issues or series have been made and designated "FRACTIONAL CURRENCY," the notes differing from those of all former issues in color, design, and paper.

Denominations.

The denominations which have been issued are 3 cents, 5 cents, 10 cents, 15 cents, 25 cents, and 50 cents. The "postage currency" had no 3-cent note, that denomination being first introduced under the act of 1863. The act of March 3, 1865, chapter 100, section 3, prohibited the issue of fractional notes of a less denomination than five cents, and required those outstanding to be redeemed and canceled. The act of May 6, 1866, chapter 81, section 3, prohibited the issue of fractional notes of a less denomination than ten cents, and required those outstanding to be retained when paid into the Treasury and canceled. The 3-cent and 5-cent notes have ceased to be printed, and those paid in have not been reissued since the passage of those acts. The 15-cent note was introduced in 1869, and belongs to the now latest series. The new fractional currency now issued is printed on the distinctive paper made expressly for the Department, and differs also from all former issues in the size, color, style, and details of the engraving.

Printed on distinctive paper.

Not a legal tender, but exchangeable for notes, and receivable for public dues.

"The notes for parts of a dollar were never declared to be lawful money or a legal tender." *Lane County* v. *Oregon*, (7 *Wallace*, 75.) But they are "exchangeable for United States notes in sums not less than three dollars, and receivable in payment of all dues to the United States less than five dollars, except customs," by the terms of the laws and the language of the notes.

Amount kept in circulation.

Within the fifty millions of dollars limited by each of the acts of 1863 and 1864, the amount kept in circulation is determined wholly by the wants and demands of the public, who, it appears, require fractional currency in the proportion of about one dollar to each inhabitant of the country. The amount in circulation rarely goes above that proportion, making proper allowance for lost and destroyed notes, and when it falls much below, a scarcity is sensibly felt throughout the country.

4.

## DISTINCTIVE PAPER FOR NOTES, BONDS, &c.

Penal offense to have in one's possession, &c., the distinctive paper used for printing notes.

The act of June 30, 1864, chapter 172, section 11, makes it a penal offense for any person to "have or retain in his custody or possession, after a distinctive paper shall have been adopted by the Secretary of the Treasury for obligations and other securities of the United States, any similar paper adapted to the making of any such obligation or other security," without authority.

All United States notes, fractional currency, and bonds of the funded loan and other obligations are now printed on distinctive paper, manufactured under the inspection of officers of the Treasury Department, at a mill exclusively employed for that purpose. Upon adopting this paper the Secretary of the Treasury published the following circular notice:

WASHINGTON, D. C., *July* 21, 1869.

Notice of the adoption of a distinctive paper.

Notice is hereby given that the Secretary of the Treasury, by authority of law, has adopted a distinctive paper, which will be hereafter used, until otherwise ordered, for all obligations and other securities of the United States.

One of its peculiarities is the introduction of colored silk, cotton, or other fibrous material into the body of the paper while in the process of manufacture.

By the laws of the United States it is made a felony for any person to have or retain in his custody or possession any paper adapted to the making of any such obligations or securities, and similar to that designated by the Secretary of the Treasury, except under authority of the Secretary of the Treasury, or some other proper officer of the United States; and any person offending against the statute will, on conviction thereof, be punished by a fine not exceeding five thousand dollars, or by imprisonment and confinement at hard labor not exceeding fifteen years, or both, in the discretion of the court.

GEO. S. BOUTWELL,
*Secretary of the Treasury.*

Another peculiarity.

Another peculiarity, and perhaps the most important and distinctive one, is the localizing of blue fibres in the body of the paper, or the introduction of blue fibres in parallel lines of about two inches in width and about three and a half inches apart, in addition to the fibres of other colors distributed throughout the paper.

## 5.

## REGULATIONS AND INSTRUCTIONS FOR REDEMPTION OF MUTILATED AND DEFACED CURRENCY.

The Treasury Department is desirous of withdrawing from circulation all notes issued prior to 1869, as well as all mutilated and defaced notes and fractional currency, and of keeping in circulation throughout the country clean new currency of the latest issue, and has adopted the following regulations and instructions on that subject, and in relation to the redemption of fragmentary notes and the distribution of new currency of the different denominations and of the most recent issue:

All defaced notes and issues prior to 1869 to be withdrawn.

### I. *Defaced and mutilated currency.*

1. Defaced and mutilated United States and fractional notes, each equaling or exceeding by face measurement three-fifths of its original proportions in one piece, if clearly genuine, are redeemable at the full face value of whole notes, in new currency, by the Treasurer, the several Assistant Treasurers, and Depositaries of the United States, and all National Bank Depositaries, and are receivable at their full face value by all officers of the Treasury Department in payment of currency dues to the United States.

What notes are redeemable at face value, and how.

2. The officers and Bank Depositaries by whom such currency is received will not use it in their disbursements, but will forward it to the Treasurer of the United States at Washington at the expense of the Department, under the Government contract with Adams Express Company.

Defaced notes not to be used by depositaries, &c.

3. Whenever the amount presented for redemption at one time to an Assistant Treasurer, Depository, or Bank Depositary equals or exceeds fifty dollars in United States notes, or five dollars in fractional currency, it is optional with the officer or bank to either pay the owner its value in new currency, or give a receipt conditioned for such payment when return for the amount has been received from the Treasurer.

When redeemed, how payable.

When the same person habitually presents currency for redemption in sums somewhat less than those mentioned, it is discretionary with the officer or bank to refuse to receive it until it has been made up to the required amount.

4

Department pays expenses of transportation to Washington.

4. The Department will receive at its own expense, under the contract with Adams Express Company, from any person, company, firm, bank, or corporation, United States notes and fractional currency which are defaced or mutilated, or in any way unfit for circulation, provided that the fractional currency be sent in sums of five dollars and upwards, and the United States notes in sums of fifty dollars and upwards. Parties remitting currency for redemption, and especially officers of the department, are, however, requested to make their remittances as large as practicable, and, when it is possible, to remit in sums of one thousand dollars or an even multiple thereof.

United States notes and fractional currency may be forwarded in the same package at the expense of the Department if at least five dollars in fractional currency is inclosed, or if the amount of the whole remittance equals or exceeds fifty dollars.

—desires to withdraw from circulation defaced notes, &c.

5. The Department is desirous of withdrawing from circulation all United States notes issued prior to the issue of 1869, whether mutilated or defaced or not, and will redeem them on the same terms and in the same manner as notes unfit for circulation.

Fractional currency to be assorted, &c.

6. Fractional currency, before being presented for redemption, must be assorted into the different issues; each issue must be assorted by denominations and inclosed in paper straps at least one inch wide, securely fastened; each strap, if the amount of the parcel will admit, must contain one hundred notes of the same denomination; and on each strap must be written with ink the number of pieces and the denomination inclosed, and the name of the owner. The entire amount must be securely done up in one package, and upon the wrapper the date, the amount inclosed, and the name of the owner must be written with ink.

II. *Fragmentary notes.*

Fragmentary notes, how redeemed.

1. Fragments of United States notes and fractional currency, constituting less than three-fifths of the original proportions of the notes, and notes torn or cut into pieces each less than three-fifths, are redeemable only by the Treasurer of the United States.

—when less than half.

2. Fragments less than half are redeemed only when accompanied by an affidavit that the missing portions have been totally destroyed. The affidavit must state the cause and the manner of the mutilation, and the character of the affiant must be certified to be good by a magistrate or other public officer. When accompanied by satisfactory proof,

such fragments will be redeemed at the full face value of the notes of which they are part.

3. Fragments each less than half, but together purporting to constitute more than one-half of a note, are redeemed only when it appears, either from the notes themselves or from an affidavit made in conformity to the foregoing paragraph, that they are actually parts of one original note. —same.

4. Fragments constituting half or more than half, but less than three-fifths of notes, when unaccompanied by evidence that the missing portions have been destroyed, are redeemable for half of the face value of the notes. —when half and less than three-fifths.

5. In redeeming, under the last preceding regulation, interest notes, with which interest is payable, half of the interest due on the notes will be paid. Interest on fragmentary notes bearing interest.

6. Demand notes are redeemable in coin by the Treasurer, on presentation at his office, on the same terms as to mutilations as United States notes. Rules apply to old demand notes.

7. Unredeemed fragments less than half are retained by the Treasurer; counterfeit notes are branded and returned. Unredeemed fragments retained; counterfeit notes returned.

III. *Mode of transmission to Treasurer.*

When a person making a remittance, either by mail or by express, fails to give his full name and post-office address, including the State, the remittance is retained until the name and address are furnished, together with a satisfactory description of the package claimed. Mode of transmission to Treasurer.

An inventory, describing the contents by parcels, denominations, and amounts, should accompany every remittance.

IV. *Remittances by express.*

1. All remittances for redemption should be addressed to the Treasurer of the United States, Washington, D. C. —by express.

2. The packages should be put up in wrappers of stout paper or cloth, tied with strong twine, secured by careful sealing, and plainly marked on the outside with the amount and nature of the contents, the full name and post-office address of the consignor, and the fact that they are forwarded under the Government contract with Adams Express Company. Packages, how put up.

3. A letter of advice, written on not less than half a sheet of commercial note paper, must be put inside the package, and a duplicate letter should be sent by mail to the Treasurer on the day that the remittance is forwarded. —accompanied with letter.

V. *Remittances by mail.*

1. All remittances by mail for redemption should be addressed to the Treasurer of the United States, Washington, Remittances by mail.

D. C. Letters or packages so addressed are forwarded without charge for postage, whether they contain money or not.

—how sealed up, &c.

2. Money for redemption, after being prepared as hereinbefore directed, should be sealed or tied up in paper of suitable strength, and plainly marked on the outside with the owner's name and full address, and with the amount inclosed. The package should then be sealed up in an envelope, together with a letter of advice, written on not less than half a sheet of commercial note paper, stating the name and full post-office address of the owner, the value of the remittance, and the manner in which return shall be made.

Remittances by mail are at risk of owners.

3. Remittances to the Treasurer by mail are invariably at the risk of the owners. All communications to the Treasurer, in regard to packages ascertained to have been lost in transmission by mail, are referred for investigation to the Second Assistant Postmaster General, to whom any further inquiry on the subject should be addressed.

4. It is a protection against loss to register letters containing money; but the registry fee must in all cases be prepaid by the party remitting.

VI. *Returns, how made.*

Return of new notes or checks, how made.

1. Returns for amounts less than five dollars are usually made in new currency by mail at the owner's risk, but if he so requests, returns are made by check on any of the cities named below, or in new currency by express at his expense.

—how usually made.

2. Returns for amounts of five dollars and upwards, received by mail, are usually made by transfer checks on the Assistant Treasurer of the United States in New York, Boston, Philadelphia, New Orleans, or San Francisco, as the owner may request; but if the owner desires new currency, it will be forwarded by express, on the terms stated in the next paragraph.

Same subject.

3. Returns for amounts of five dollars and upwards in fractional currency, and fifty dollars and upwards in United States notes, are ordinarily made in new currency by express, at the expense of the Department; but if the owner requests it, a check on any of the above-mentioned Assistant Treasurers will be sent. Returns for five, or more than five but less than fifty dollars, in United States notes, are ordinarily made by check; but new currency is returned by express, at the owner's expense, whenever he requests it.

Proceeds from Government officers credited to their accounts if desired.

4. The proceeds of remittances from Assistant Treasurers, Designated Depositaries, and other officers of the Government, and National Bank depositaries, are, when they so request, credited in account.

VII. *General Instructions.*

1. Every officer of the Treasury Department is required, whenever any spurious note purporting to have been issued by the United States is presented to him, to write or stamp on it the word "Counterfeit."

Spurious notes to be stamped.

2. Notes of National Banks that have failed or gone into voluntary liquidation are received, redeemed, and forwarded to the Treasurer by the officers and banks before-mentioned for retirement under these rules, in the same manner and on the same terms as United States notes of issues prior to 1869. Notes of all other National Banks, whether mutilated or not, are redeemable only by the banks which issued them and by their redeeming agents.

Notes of failed banks, how redeemed.

3. In case of the loss or destruction of one of his checks, and of an application for a duplicate, the Treasurer stops payment of the original check, and furnishes the applicant for a duplicate with a form of bond of indemnity, upon return of which, properly executed, a duplicate is issued.

Payment of lost checks may be stopped.

VIII. *New fractional currency.*

In addition to being forwarded, when desired, in return for old, defaced, and mutilated currency, on the terms already mentioned, new fractional currency is forwarded by express from the Treasurer's office, under the Government contract with Adams Express Company, in sums of even thousands of dollars—

New fractional currency, how obtained from the Treasurer.

1. On the receipt of original certificates of deposit to the Treasurer's credit, issued by Assistant Treasurers and Designated Depositaries of the United States and National Bank Depositaries; and

2. On the receipt and collection of drafts on banks and bankers in Boston, New York, Philadelphia, and Washington.

If the amount applied for is less than one thousand dollars, the express charges at contract rates are deducted from the remittance; if less than an even multiple of one thousand dollars, the charges on the fractional part of one thousand dollars included in the amount are deducted.

IX. *Government contract with Adams Express Company.*

1. The Government contract with Adams Express Company extends to and includes all "points accessible through established express lines, reached by continuous railway connection," within the United States, but does not extend westward beyond Omaha and Nebraska City, in Nebraska, and Atchison and Leavenworth, in Kansas, nor include the

Contract with express company for transporting notes, &c.

lines of Wells, Fargo & Co., in Missouri and Iowa. The contract covers the lines of the following express companies: Adams, American Merchants' Union, Central, Earl, Eastern, Harnden, Hope,. Howard, National, New Jersey, Southern, Union, United States, and United States and Canada. Remittances can be made by express by private parties, at the expense of the Department, only from points within the territory covered by the contract.

# CHAPTER IV.

REGISTERED AND COUPON BONDS, HOW TRANSFERRED; ISSUE OF DUPLICATES IN CASE OF LOSS OR DESTRUCTION; CONVERSION OF BONDS; PAYMENT OF INTEREST.



## 1.

## REGISTERED BONDS OR STOCK, HOW ASSIGNED.

These bonds, without coupons attached, are made payable to the person or persons named therein, who alone can collect the interest thereon and the principal when payable, and are transferable only on the books of the Register of the Treasury, in accordance with the following rules and instructions of the Treasury Department: Registered bonds. How assigned.

*Transfer of stock or registered bonds.*

Stock to be transferred, when properly perfected, should be transmitted to the REGISTER OF THE TREASURY, accompanied by an explicit letter of instructions, giving the official title of the loan; the date of the authorizing act; the number and amount of each certificate; the name of the assignee, *plainly written;* his place of residence, giving the number of the house, the name of the street, and the city or town, county, and State; the denomination of the certificates desired in exchange; and the depository at which the interest is to be made payable. Rules and regulations for transfer.

If stock of different loans is sent at the same time, a separate letter must accompany each issue or series, like the following form:

*Form of letter.*

NEW YORK, *August* 10, 1872.

Form of letter.

To the REGISTER OF THE TREASURY:

Herewith find $20,000 registered stock, CONSOLS of 1868, act of March 3, 1865, viz:

|  |  |  |  |
|---|---|---|---|
| No. 13,921 | $500 | No. 2,112 | $1,000 |
| 13,987 | 500 | 813 | 5,000 |
| 6,232 | 1,000 | 1,627 | 10,000 |
| 6,409 | 1,000 | | |
| 6,101 | 1,000 | | $20,000 |

Which please register in two $10,000 certificates in the name of Jno. Henry Brown, of No. 23 Waverly street, Chicago, Cook county, Illinois, making the interest payable at the United States Depository, Chicago, Illinois.

Very respectfully, JNO. HENRY BROWN.

*New certificates.*

New certificates.

The certificates forwarded for transfer are canceled, and new ones issued in the name of the assignee.

The new certificate bears interest from the first day of the quarter or half year (as the interest may be payable) in which the transfer is made.

The new certificate is usually returned the same day the old is received, and is invariably sent *by mail* to the party forwarding the assigned certificate, unless otherwise positively instructed.

If the certificate is sent by express, it must be at the cost of the party so ordering.

*Closing of the transfer books.*

Closing of the transfer books.

For the purpose of preparing the interest schedules, the transfer books are closed for thirty days on all loans except the Funded Loan of 1881, and on this latter for fifteen days, immediately preceding interest day. The dates of closing are as follows:

Loan of 1858—June 1st and December 1st.
Loan of February, 1861—June 1st and December 1st.
Loan of July, 1861—June 1st and December 1st.
Five-twenties of 1862—April 1st and October 1st.
Loan of 1863—June 1st and December 1st.
Ten-forties of 1864—February 1st and August 1st.
Five-twenties of March, 1864—April 1st and October 1st.
Five-twenties of June, 1864—April 1st and October 1st.
Five-twenties of 1865—April 1st and October 1st.

Consols of 1865—June 1st and December 1st.
Consols of 1867—June 1st and December 1st.
Consols of 1868—June 1st and December 1st.
Funded loan of 1881—January 15, April 15, July 15, and October 15.
Pacific Railway stock—June 1st and December 1st.

If stock to be transferred is not received previous to the day for closing the transfer books, the dividend will be declared to the party whose name appears upon the face of the certificate and the record, and the assignee must look to him for the accrued interest for that quarter or half year. **Who entitled to interest when bonds assigned after books closed.**

*Form of assignment.*

The printed form on the back of the certificate should be carefully followed, and all the blanks filled. **Form of assignments.**

The name of the assignee should be plainly written in full in the blank space for that purpose.

If the certificate is to be divided among two or more persons, their names and the amount to each should be plainly indicated in the assignment. If only a part of the certificate is assigned, a new certificate for the remainder will be issued to the former payee.

Certificates should never be assigned in blank, as this gives them the character of coupon bonds, and they are then transferable by delivery.

A detached assignment, where no assignment appears on the bond, should never be used, as it invites fraud or forgery should the certificate fall into improper hands.

*Assignments by representatives of deceased persons.*

In case of death or successorship, the representative or successor must furnish official evidence of decease and appointment. **Assignments by representatives of deceased persons.**

An executor or administrator may assign stock standing in the name of a deceased person.

Where there is more than one legal representative, all must unite in the assignment, unless by a decree of court or provision of will some one is designated to dispose of the stock.

If the stock was held by the deceased as a fiduciary, the letters of administration must be accompanied by an order of the court, authorizing the transfer.

*Assignments in foreign countries.*

Where the payee at the time of his death was a resident of a foreign country, the person claiming to direct the **—in foreign countries.**

transfer must produce an exemplified copy of the will or other instrument conferring the authority, duly certified under the hand and seal of the proper officer, attested by the certificate of a United States minister, chargé, consul, vice consul, or commercial agent, or, if there be none, by a notary public, to the effect that such exemplified copy is granted by the proper officer or tribunal, and is in due form, and according to the laws of the country. The assignment should be executed as hereinbefore directed.

*Execution of assignments.*

Execution of assignments.

The payee should sign his name to the assignment as it is written in the face of the certificate.

If issued to a firm, it must be signed by a member authorized to sign the firm-name, of which authority the person witnessing must be satisfied; if to joint owners, co-trustees, executors, administrators, or guardians, each person must sign for himself; if to a corporation or company, the official character of the person signing, and his authority to dispose of the stock, should be duly attested by vote or resolution of the board of directors, or its equivalent, certified under seal.

Where an officer is authorized to assign by virtue of his office, a certificate of the fact and of his election must be furnished, under seal, together with a certified copy of the by-laws. All such certificates are placed on file for reference in future transactions, and need not be repeated if properly referred to.

The following form of authority may be used:

*Form of authority by vote.*

Form of authority by vote.

At a meeting of the Board of Directors of the National Savings Institution of Washington, D. C., held July 10, 1872, it was, on motion,

*Resolved*, That James Jones, President, and Henry Smith, Treasurer, or either of them, are hereby authorized and empowered to assign any and all United States stock now standing [*or which may hereafter stand*] in the name of this institution.

I certify that the above is a true copy from the minutes.

[Corporate seal.] Henry Smith,
*Treasurer and Secretary of Board.*

*Form of vote under by-laws.*

—under by-laws.

At the annual meeting of the stockholders of the Treasury National Bank of Washington, D. C., held July 1,

1872, John Doe was duly elected President, and Richard Roe Cashier, and, as such, are jointly or severally empowered by the by-laws (a certified copy of which is hereto annexed) to sell and assign any and all United States stock now standing, or which may hereafter stand, in the name of this bank.

Attest: RICHARD ROE, *Cashier.*

[Seal of bank.]

*Acknowledgment of assignment.*

Acknowledgments of assignments, when not made at the Department, must be before an Assistant Treasurer, Designated Depositary, United States judge, district attorney, clerk of a United States court, or collector of customs, but a notary public is authorized to take acknowledgments on all loans except the Funded Loan of 1881, and on this loan the president or cashier of a National Bank is authorized.

Acknowledgment of assignment.

The witness must, in all cases, append his official title, and affix his seal of office, if he has one. The president or cashier of a National Bank must affix the title of the bank.

*Acknowledgment in foreign countries.*

Acknowledgments in foreign countries may be made before a United States minister, chargé, consul, vice consul, or commercial agent. A notary public, or other equivalent officer, in a foreign country, may take acknowledgments, but his official character must be properly verified. The official seal, where there is one, should in all cases be affixed.

—in foreign countries.

*Powers of attorney to assign stock.*

Persons entitled to assign stock may appoint an attorney for that purpose, who, by virtue of the authority so conferred, can execute the assignment in the same manner as provided for the constituent. No officer of the Treasury should be selected as attorney. The following form may be used:

Powers of attorney to assign stock.

*Form of power.*

KNOW ALL MEN BY THESE PRESENTS, That I, John Doe, do hereby appoint Richard Roe my attorney, to sell and assign all United States stock now standing [*or which may hereafter stand*] in my name on the books of the Treasury Department, granting to said attorney full power to appoint one or more substitutes for that purpose, hereby ratifying and confirming all that may be lawfully done by virtue hereof.

—form of.

Witness my hand and seal this 9th day of July, A. D. 1872.

JOHN DOE. [Seal of wax or wafer.]

Executed before me this 10th day of July, A. D. 1872.

[Official seal.]

JOHN JONES,
*Collector of Customs, Chicago, Ill.*

*Power to collect interest.*

—to collect interest.

Powers to collect interest should follow the same general form.

*Acknowledgment of powers.*

—acknowledgment of.

Powers of attorney for the transfer of stock or the collection of interest must be acknowledged in the presence of some one of the officers authorized to take acknowledgments of assignments. Where any such officer has an official seal, it must be affixed.

*Powers of substitution.*

Powers of substitution.

Powers of substitution must be executed and acknowledged in the same manner as powers of attorney, and should follow the same general form.

*No fees.*

No fees chargable for assignments.

No fees will be charged by a United States minister, chargé, consul, vice consul, or commercial agent for witnessing and certifying an assignment or power to assign stock or collect interest thereon. No charge is made by the Department for transferring certificates or for changing coupon bonds into registered stock.

*Papers in foreign languages.*

Papers in foreign languages must be translated.

Powers of attorney, and all other papers executed in the United States, must be in the English language. If executed abroad in any other language, an accurate English translation must accompany each.

## 2.

## LOST OR DESTROYED REGISTERED BONDS.

Notice of lost registered bonds should be given to Treasury Department.

Owners of lost or stolen *registered* bonds should give notice of the fact of the loss or larceny, as soon as known to them, to the Treasury Department at Washington, D. C., in order that innocent persons may be saved, if possible, from loss by forged or fraudulent assignments on the back of the certificates.

When a caveated registered bond is sent in for transfer, the Treasury Department retains and holds it for the rightful owner, to whom notice of the fact is immediately given, and at the same time notice that the assignment is supposed or claimed to be fraudulent is sent to the person from whom it was received, that he may institute measures to trace out the parties to the fraud; but the Department does not undertake, by detectives or otherwise, to discover the guilty persons.

Whether or not any particular bond has been caveated may be ascertained, if the genuine number is known, by writing to the Secretary of the Treasury for information.

Duplicates of lost or destroyed registered bonds.

Owners of lost or destroyed *registered* bonds may obtain duplicates thereof by complying with the provisions of the following law of Congress, passed for that purpose:

JOINT RESOLUTION TO ENABLE OWNERS TO OBTAIN DUPLICATES OF LOST AND DESTROYED REGISTERED BONDS OF THE UNITED STATES.

Law of Congress.

*Resolved by the Senate and House of Representatives of the United States of America in Congress assembled*, That the Secretary of the Treasury be, and hereby is, authorized and directed, whenever it is proved by clear and satisfactory evidence that any duly registered bond of the United States, bearing interest, issued for valuable consideration in pursuance of law, has been lost or destroyed, so that the same is not held by any person as his own property, to issue a duplicate of said registered bond, to be so marked, of like amount, and bearing like interest as the bond so proved to be lost or destroyed:

*Provided*, That the owner of such missing bond shall file in the Treasury a bond in a penal sum equal to the amount of said missing bond, and the interest which would accrue thereon, until the principal thereof is due and payable, with two good and sufficient sureties, residents of the United States, to the approval of the Secretary of the Treasury, with condition to indemnify and save harmless the United States from any claim because of the said lost or destroyed bond.

*Approved March* 3, 1871.

Regulations respecting lost certificates.

The regulations and instructions of the Treasury Department in relation to lost certificates are as follows:

*Lost certificates.*

Caveating lost certificates.

The Secretary of the Treasury should be immediately notified of the loss of any certificate of registered stock, that a caveat may be entered against its transfer.

The notice should give the number and amount of the certificate; the official title of the loan; the date of the authorizing act; and the name and address of the registered payee.

If the stock is not recovered within a reasonable time, a duplicate will be issued, under the regulations hereinafter prescribed.

The law does not authorize the issue of duplicates in lieu of lost coupon bonds.

The following form of caveat may be used:

*Form of caveat.*

Form of caveat.

NEW YORK CITY, *August* 1, 1872.

To the SECRETARY OF THE TREASURY:

Please take notice that certificates of registered stock—-

No. 2310 for $10,000, Loan of July, 1861, acts of July 17 and August 5, 1861;

903 for $5,000, Loan of 1863, act of March 3, 1863;

1220 for $5,000, Five-twenties of 1865, act of March 3, 1865;

1920 for $10,000, Funded Loan of 1881, acts of July 14, 1870, and January 20, 1871,

were stolen from the undersigned on or about the 25th day of July last. Please enter a caveat against their transfer. The registered payee of the first one was Jno. Doe, of No. 25 River street, Troy, N. Y., and of the other three,

Respectfully, yours, RICHARD ROE,
*Of No.* 9 *Park Place, New York City.*

*Duplicates, how obtained.*

Duplicates, how obtained.

In case a lost certificate of registered stock cannot be recovered, the payee should furnish the Secretary of the Treasury with an affidavit, duly authenticated, showing the number and amount of the certificate; the official title of the loan; the date of the authorizing act; the name and address of the registered payee; the name of the assignor and assignee; the time and place of purchase; of whom purchased; the consideration paid; and the material facts and circumstances attending the loss.

On receipt of this affidavit, with such additional evidence as the payee may be able to furnish, the case will be referred to the proper officer for his decision.

As soon as a favorable conclusion is reached, a bond of indemnity in double the amount of the lost certificate will be prepared and forwarded for execution; and upon its return, executed in conformity to instructions, the duplicate will be issued.

In all cases, and especially where there are conflicting claimants, proofs should be made as full and clear as possible, that the title be so proved as to leave no doubt of the good faith of the holder or claimant.

The following form of affidavit may be used:

*Form of affidavit.*

Form of affidavit.

Personally appeared before me, a notary public in and for the county of Cook, and State of Illinois, the subscriber, John Doe, who, being duly sworn according to law, deposes and says: That he was the lawful owner of one certificate of registered stock of the United States, numbered two hundred and three, (203,) for ten thousand (10,000) dollars, Consols of 1868, act of March 3, 1865, registered at the Treasury of the United States in the name of Richard Roe, now residing at number two hundred and nine (209) South Clark street, in the city of Chicago, and State of Illinois; that the said certificate was indorsed to me by the said Richard Roe, all the blanks thereon being properly filled out, and the transfer witnessed by John Smith, United States district attorney for the northern district of Illinois; that said stock was purchased at Chicago, Illinois, on or about the 15th day of July, A. D. 1872, of the said Richard Roe; that the consideration paid therefor was eleven thousand two hundred (11,200) dollars, lawful money of the United States; that the said certificate was stolen from the vault of the Ninth National Bank of the City of Chicago, on the night of the 20th of July, A. D. 1872, by some person or persons unknown to me; and that due diligence has been exercised in endeavoring to recover the same, without success.

JOHN DOE,
*Of No.* 23 *West Lake street*, *Chicago*, *Ill.*

Sworn and subscribed before me this 1st day of August, A. D. 1872.

JOHN JONES,
*Notary Public.*

[Notarial seal.]

*Destroyed or mutilated bonds, whether registered or coupon.*

Destroyed or mutilated bonds, whether registered or coupon.

Parties presenting claims on account of coupon or registered bonds, which have been destroyed in whole or in part, must furnish the same evidence as in the case of lost bonds, and, in addition, must state whether the bonds were coupon or registered.

—same subject.

Duplicates of bonds which are mutilated, defaced, or indorsed, so as to be unsaleable, may be obtained under another law hereinafter set forth without giving a bond of indemnity. (*See page* 68.)

3.

COUPON BONDS, HOW TRANSFERRED.

Coupon bonds.

These bonds, with the semi-annual or quarter-annual coupons attached, are payable to bearer, and the legal title thereto passes by delivery, like bank bills and legal-tender notes. The Government pays them to the bearer who holds them in good faith, without investigating how previous holders acquired their title.

The Supreme Court of the United States has recognized and settled the following principles as applicable to coupon bonds:

Decisions of the courts as to transfer of bonds before maturity.

"The possession of such paper carries the title with it to the holder. 'The possession and title are one and inseparable.' The party who takes it before due for a valuable consideration, without knowledge of any defect of title, and in good faith, holds it by a title valid against all the world. Suspicion of defect of title, or the knowledge of circumstances which would excite such suspicion in the mind of a prudent man, or gross negligence on the part of the taker at the time of the transfer, will not defeat his title. That result can be produced only by bad faith on his part. The burden of proof lies on the person who assails the right claimed by the party in possession. Such is the settled law of this court, and we feel no disposition to depart from it." (*Murray* v. *Lardner*, 2 *Wallace*, 110; *Thomson* v. *Lee County*, 3 *Wallace*, 327; *Texas* v. *White*, 7 *Wallace*, 735.)

Different rule applicable to bonds over-due.

"These rules were fully discussed in *Murray* v. *Lardner*, (cited above.) We held in that case that the purchaser of coupon bonds before due, without notice and in good faith, is unaffected by want of title in the seller, and that the burden of proof, in respect to notice and want of good faith, is on the claimant of the bonds as against the purchaser. We are entirely satisfied with this doctrine." "But these rules have never been applied to matured obligations.

Purchasers of notes or bonds past due take nothing but the actual right and title of the vendors. The bonds in question were dated January 1, 1851, and were redeemable after the 31st of December, 1864. In strictness, it is true they were not payable on the day when they became redeemable; but the known usage of the United States to pay all bonds as soon as the right of payment accrues, except where a distinction between redeemability and payability is made by law, and shown on the face of the bonds, requires the application of the rule respecting over-due obligations to bonds of the United States which have become redeemable, and in respect to which no such distinction has been made." (*Texas* v. *White*, 7 *Wallace*, 735; *Texas* v. *Hardenberg*, 10 *Wallace*, 68.)

The Supreme Judicial Court of Massachusetts has made the following decision as to the title of holders of coupons: Title of holders of coupons.

"But in the opinion of a majority of the court the coupons in question do not stand upon the same ground as chattels. They were negotiable promises for the payment of money, issued by the Government, payable to bearer and transferable by mere delivery, without assignment or indorsement. They are therefore not to be considered as goods, but as representatives of money, and subject to the same rules as bank bills or other negotiable instruments payable in money to bearer. The rule of *caveat emptor* does not apply to them. It is now well settled that the bearer of a bank bill which has been stolen from the bank may recover the amount from the bank, unless it is proved that he did not take it in good faith and for a valuable consideration; and that his knowledge of suspicious circumstances is immaterial, unless amounting to proof of want of good faith." (*Spooner* v. *Holmes*, 102 *Mass.*, 503.)

And the Supreme Court of the United States has declared that— Coupons detached from bonds.

"Bonds with coupons, payable to bearer, are negotiable securities, and pass by delivery, and in fact have all the qualities and incidents of commercial paper. It is not necessary that the holder of coupons, in order to recover on them, should own the bonds from which they are detached. The coupons are drawn so that they can be separated from the bonds, and, like the bonds, are negotiable; and the owner of them can sue, without the production of the bonds to which they are attached, or without being interested in them." (*Thomson* v. *Lee County*, 3 *Wallace*, 331.)

4.

## DESTROYED AND DEFACED BONDS.

Caveats of lost and stolen bonds.

Persons often forward to the Treasury Department caveats of lost and stolen *coupon* bonds, but the only advantage gained thereby is, that when those bonds, or the coupons, come in for redemption, the Department notifies the claimants who have filed the caveats of the presentation of the bonds, and furnishes the names of the parties presenting them, in order that the loser may have all the information within the reach of the Government which may possibly enable him to discover the parties who fraudulently obtained them. Beyond this the Government can afford no relief.

Numbers, &c., of bonds should be taken and kept by holders.

There are great advantages in holders carefully taking the numbers, dates, denominations, issues, and series of their coupon bonds, and preserving them in some place apart from the bonds themselves; because in case of *destruction* of the bonds, by fire or otherwise, duplicates may be obtained under a law of Congress passed June 1, 1872, and unless such memoranda are kept, it is difficult, if not impossible, to describe coupon bonds which have been destroyed, with sufficient accuracy to obtain the benefits of the law. The facts as to the title of registered stock, but not as to coupon bonds, may be gathered from the records of the Department.

Defaced and destroyed bonds.

The following is the law for the issue of duplicates of destroyed or defaced bonds:

AN ACT TO PROVIDE FOR THE ISSUE OF BONDS IN LIEU OF DESTROYED OR DEFACED BONDS OF THE UNITED STATES.

*Be it enacted by the Senate and House of Representatives of the United States of America in Congress assembled*, That whenever it shall appear to the Secretary of the Treasury, by clear and unequivocal proof, that any interest-bearing bond of the United States has, without bad faith upon the part of the owner, been destroyed, wholly or in part, or so defaced as to impair its value to the holder, and which bond shall be identified by number and description, the Secretary of the Treasury shall, under such regulations and with such restrictions as to time and retention for security or otherwise as he may prescribe, issue a duplicate of such bond, having the same time to run, bearing like interest as the bond so proved to have been destroyed or defaced, and so marked as to show the original number of the bond destroyed and the date thereof:

*Provided*, That where such destroyed or defaced bonds shall appear to have been of such a class or series as has been or may, before such application, be called in for redemption, instead of issuing duplicates thereof they shall be paid, with such interest only as would have been paid if presented in accordance with such call.

SEC. 2. That the owner of such destroyed or defaced bond shall surrender the same, or so much thereof as may remain, and shall file in the Treasury a bond in a penal sum double the amount of said destroyed or defaced bond, and the interest which would accrue thereon until the principal thereof is due and payable, with two good and sufficient sureties, residents of the United States, to be approved by the Secretary of the Treasury, with condition to indemnify and save harmless the United States from any claim upon the said destroyed or defaced bond.

*Approved June* 1, 1872.

This act applies to both registered and coupon bonds, while the act of March 3, 1871, printed on page 61, applies only to those which are registered.

Applies to regis- and coupon bonds.

The regulations and instructions of the Treasury Department for the issue of duplicate bonds under the foregoing act are the same as those under the law for the issue of duplicates of lost *registered bonds*, which are set forth in full on pages 61–64. Those instructions must be carefully followed, specifying, however, whether the bonds are coupon or registered.

Regulations and instructions.

It will be seen that the law makes no provision for the issue of duplicates of *lost coupon bonds*, as it does of those which are registered, for the reason that the former are payable to bearer and pass by delivery, and the *bona fide* holders acquire a legal title thereto; while as to the latter, the lost registered bond, like a certificate of shares in a corporation, only designates the owner, and the record of it in the Register's office, where alone it can be transferred, is still evidence of the payee's title.

Duplicates of lost coupon bonds not provided for.

Duplicates of defaced bonds.

The foregoing act, so far as it relates to defaced bonds, seems to apply especially to tho e which are defaced or mutilated under such circumstances or in such manner as to excite suspicions of their genuineness, or as to render it possible that there may be other claimants thereto. The provisions of the last clause of section 7 of the act of June 30, 1864, chapter 172, were sufficient to authorize the issue of duplicates for bonds which were so mutilated, defaced, or indorsed as simply to render their acceptance by purchasers in the market somewhat objectionable, on account of the appearance of the bonds, but without raising any suspicions against their genuineness or the title of the holder thereto. That law is as follows:

SEC. 7. *And be it further enacted,* That * * * * And for all mutilated, defaced, or indorsed coupon or other bonds presented to the Department, the Secretary of the Treasury is authorized to issue, upon terms and under regulations as aforesaid, and in substitution therefor, other bonds of like or equivalent issues.

When new bonds are issued under this act as a substitute for those which are mutilated, defaced, or indorsed, no bond of indemnity is required. If any part of the bonds are missing, duplicates can be obtained only under the laws and regulations hereinbefore set forth.

## 5.

## CONVERSION OF COUPON BONDS TO REGISTERED STOCK.

Conversion of coupon to registered bonds.

Under the following law holders of coupon bonds can have the same converted into registered stock of the same loan, without any charge therefor, by transmitting them to the Secretary of the Treasury at their own expense and requesting such exchange; but registered stock cannot be converted into coupon bonds:

ACT OF JUNE 30, 1864, CHAPTER 172.

Law of Congress.

SEC. 7. *And be it further enacted,* That the Secretary of the Treasury is hereby authorized to issue, upon such terms and under such regulations as he may from time to time prescribe, registered bonds in exchange for, and in lieu of, any coupon bonds which have been or may hereafter be lawfully issued; such registered bonds to be similar in all respects to the registered bonds issued under the acts authorizing the issue of the coupon bonds offered for exchange.

6.

## PAYMENT OF INTEREST ON REGISTERED STOCK.

The following are the rules of the Treasury Department in relation to the payment of interest on registered bonds: Interest on registered bonds.

*Payment of interest.*

Holders of registered stock of all loans but the funded loan of 1881, must select one of the following offices at which to receive their interest. —where payable.

It is payable to the holder on application in person or by attorney.

The place of payment will be changed on notice in writing from the holder, if sent to the Register of the Treasury before the transfer books are closed.

Dividend offices.

The Treasury of the United States at Washington, D. C.
The Assistant Treasury at Boston, Massachusetts.
The Assistant Treasury at New York, New York.
The Assistant Treasury at Philadelphia, Pennsylvania.
The Assistant Treasury at Baltimore, Maryland.
The Assistant Treasury at Charleston, South Carolina.
The Assistant Treasury at New Orleans, Louisiana.
The Assistant Treasury at St. Louis, Missouri.
The Assistant Treasury at San Francisco, California.
The Designated Depository at Buffalo, New York.
The Designated Depository at Pittsburg, Pennsylvania.
The Designated Depository at Cincinnati, Ohio.
The Designated Depository at Chicago, Illinois.

In case stock is transferred between the day for closing the dividend books and the day it becomes due, the interest is declared to the registered payee, and the purchaser must look to him for that interest. Interest on stock assigned while transfer books are closed.

On the funded loan of 1881, registered interest is payable by check of the Treasurer to the order of the holder or his attorney. Interest on funded loan payable by checks.

These checks will be sent by mail, when the correct post-office address is known, otherwise they will be held by the

Treasurer until called for. They are payable, when properly indorsed, on presentation at any one of the above-named offices.

Holders of this stock should notify the Register of the Treasury of any change in their address.

Interest on stocks of joint holders.

Interest will be paid to any one of several joint holders, or co-trustees, executors, administrators, or guardians, but in the execution of a power to a third party to collect all must join. In case of the death of either, the survivors will be recognized as having full authority, upon due proof of such death and survivorship. The same rule will govern at the final redemption of a loan.

Interest not claimed for ninety days, how collected.

If the interest on registered stock of the old loans is not claimed within ninety days after interest day, it will be returned to the Treasury as unclaimed, and must then be collected in person or by attorney, at the office of the Treasurer in Washington.

For the convenience of the public, powers to collect *specified* unclaimed interest may be made in favor of the "Chief of the Loan Division of the Secretary's office," and be sent by mail to the Secretary of the Treasury. It will then be collected, and a check for the amount will be sent by mail.

Dividend officers to deposit unclaimed interest at once, &c.

Deposits of unclaimed interest should be promptly made by the several dividend offices at the expiration of the ninety days. The certificates of deposit should specifically state why the interest is deposited, and to what loan account it belongs. If on account of several loans, the amount to each must be stated. The information must be full and explicit, and should be indorsed on the back of the original certificate, which should be at once forwarded to the Secretary of the Treasury, the depositor retaining the duplicate.

Powers of attorney to collect interest.

Powers of attorney to collect interest on registered bonds are required to be in the same general form, must be acknowledged, and are subject to the rules and instructions applicable to powers to assign and transfer certificates of stock, as given on pages 59, 60.

## 7.

## PAYMENT OF COUPONS.

Payment of coupons.

Coupons are paid by the Treasurer of the United States at Washington, by either of the Assistant Treasurers or Designated Depositaries named on page 69, where interest on registered stock is payable, and also by the Designated Depositaries at Mobile, Alabama; Louisville, Kentucky; Santa Fé, New Mexico; and Tucson, Arizona Territory, at the option of holders.

For the regulations of the Department in relation to the payment of coupons on bonds called in for redemption, when only a fractional part of the coupon is payable, *see Chapter V.*

8.

## PAYMENT OF INTEREST BEFORE MATURITY.

The Secretary of the Treasury has authority to pay, and often does pay, coupons and interest on registered stock in advance of maturity. When the time of payment is only a few days in advance, the whole amount is paid without rebate, but for longer periods of time a proportional rebate has been made. No interest is subject to rebate which is not voluntarily applied for before maturity.

**Payment of interest in advance of maturity.**

Previous public notice is always given in each case of the intention of the Government to make advance payments at any designated time.

The following is the law of Congress under which payment of interest is thus anticipated, being chapter 20 of the Resolutions of the year 1864:

**Law for advanced payments.**

JOINT RESOLUTION TO AUTHORIZE THE SECRETARY OF THE TREASURY TO ANTICIPATE THE PAYMENT OF INTEREST ON THE PUBLIC DEBT, AND FOR OTHER PURPOSES.

*Be it resolved by the Senate and House of Representatives of the United States of America in Congress assembled,* That the Secretary of the Treasury be authorized to anticipate the payment of interest on the public debt, by a period not exceeding one year, from time to time, either with or without a rebate of interest upon the coupons, as to him may seem expedient. * * * * * *

*Approved March* 17, 1864.

There is a standing order of the Treasury Department that coupons will be paid on presentation sixty days before maturity, upon a rebate of interest at the rate of six per cent. per annum in gold.

**Standing order for payment of coupons in advance on rebate of interest.**

# CHAPTER V.

## COIN IN THE TREASURY; SALE OF GOLD; PURCHASE OF BONDS; REDEMPTION OF BONDS; MONTHLY DEBT STATEMENT.



### 1.

### COIN IN THE TREASURY.

Coin kept in the Treasury.

The coin received from duties on imports has every year been more than the amount necessary for the payment of interest on the public debt and the principal of that portion which has matured during the same period, and for other disbursements of the Government required to be paid in specie; and from seventy to a hundred millions of dollars have been constantly kept in the Treasury for several years past, under different Secretaries, as a reserve, to be used at times when the exigencies of the Government should require it.

### 2.

### SALE OF GOLD AND PURCHASE OF BONDS.

Authority to sell gold.

Congress, by joint resolution of March 17, 1864, authorized the Secretary of the Treasury "to dispose of any gold in the Treasury of the United States not necessary for the payment of interest of the public debt: *Provided,* That the obligation to create the sinking fund, according to the act of February twenty-fifth, eighteen hundred and sixty-two, shall not be impaired thereby."

—to buy bonds.

And by act of July 11, 1862, chapter 142, section 1, the Secretary of the Treasury was authorized to "purchase, at rates not exceeding that of the current market and cost of purchase not exceeding one-eighth of one per centum, any bonds or certificates of debt of the United States, as he might deem advisable." The act of March 3, 1863, chapter 73, section 3, repealed so much of the act of July 11, 1862, and another act, as restricted the "negotiation of bonds" to market value, and if that applies to the *purchase* of bonds, it allows the Secretary to buy at any price.

It has been the invariable practice of the Department since March, 1869, to sell gold and purchase bonds in the open market, and only through the Assistant Treasurer at New York, on proposals invited from the public by notifications in the newspapers. Within a few days of the close of each month the Secretary sends written instructions to the Assistant Treasurer at New York as to the amount of gold to be sold and bonds to be purchased during the then next month, specifying the dates of purchases and sales, and the amounts of each.

**How gold is sold and bonds are purchased.**

The purchase of bonds always takes place on Wednesday and the sale of gold on Thursday, so that currency may be paid out of the Treasury for bonds before it is required for the payment of gold purchased.

The Assistant Treasurer publishes in the newspapers a notice inviting proposals in the following form, only varying the dates and amounts each month according to the direction of the Secretary:

**Public notice.**

OFFICE OF U. S. ASSISTANT TREASURER,
NEW YORK, *June* 3, 1872.

During the month of June, 1872, I shall, by order, receive bids for gold, and offers of bonds as follows:

| *Bids for gold.* | *Offers of bonds.* |
|---|---|
| Thursday, June 6, —— millions. | Wednesday, June 5, —— millions. |
| Thursday, June 13, —— millions. | Wednesday, June 12, —— millions. |
| Thursday, June 20, —— millions. | Wednesday, June 19, —— millions. |
| Thursday, June 27, —— millions. | Wednesday, June 26, —— millions. |

A certified check for five per cent. of bid or offer must be deposited therewith. Proposals will be opened at 12 o'clock, noon, each day specified. The Treasury may, at its option, accept offers of bonds or bids for gold in excess of the amount advertised for.

Printed forms for proposals, with regulations to be observed, will be furnished at this office.

THOMAS HILLHOUSE,
*Assistant Treasurer U. S.*

The regulations and form of proposals referred to in the notice are as follows:

*Purchase of bonds.*

Proposals must be for not less than five thousand dollars, and must state the kind of bonds offered, whether coupon or registered, and of what loan and issue.

Proposals must specify the price desired, in currency, for the principal of the bonds only, without regard to the accrued coin interest which will be paid on purchased bonds to the date of purchase.

The payment will be in United States or national bank notes, as the convenience and condition of the Treasury may warrant.

The interest on the purchased bonds will cease from the date of purchase.

Bonds purchased must be delivered, in all cases, the day following the award. In case of failure to deliver the bonds within the time specified, they will be purchased in the open market for account of the sellers.

Bonds will be received at this office and paid for, subject to examination by the Department at Washington, and if rejected the sellers will be required to substitute other acceptable bonds.

Bonds rejected by the Department as counterfeit, or for fraudulent alterations or transfers, of whatever nature, will be retained, without prejudice to the right of the Department to require the substitution therefor, by the seller, of other acceptable bonds.

Proposals must be plain, specific, and free from any erasures or alterations likely to lead to misunderstanding.

Proposals adverse to the interest of the Government will be rejected.

Each proposal must contain a certified check for five per cent. of the amount offered. When proposals are rejected, the checks will be returned as soon as the awards are determined upon. If proposals are accepted, the checks will be returned on completion of the delivery of the bonds.

In all proposals for the sale of bonds, it must be distinctly stated that they are made subject to the foregoing regulations and conditions.

Suitable forms will be furnished on application at this office.

*Sales of gold.*

Proposals must be for sums not less than five thousand dollars.

Payment may be made in lawful money or three per cent. certificates.

Each proposal must contain a certified check for five per cent. of the amount bid for.

Proposals adverse to the interest of the Government will be rejected.

The proposals will be opened at 12 M. on the days announced for purchases and sales.

The right is reserved to accept more or less than the amount advertised for, either of bonds or gold.

*Form of proposal.*

NEW YORK, ——, 187–. Form of proposal.

To the ASSISTANT TREASURER U. S.,
*New York.*

SIR: In accordance with the terms of your advertisement, and subjected to the annexed conditions, the following offer —— is submitted.

Very respectfully. —— ——.

Proposals when opened are immediately telegraphed to the Secretary of the Treasury at Washington, and the amount to be sold or purchased on each occasion is decided by him and telegraphed back to the Assistant Treasurer, who announces the same at once. Secretary determines amount of sales and purchases on each occasion.

## 3.

## PAYMENT AND REDEMPTION OF BONDS.

In the bonds of the United States a distinction is made between "redeemable" and "payable." They are "redeemable" when the Government has the option to pay them or to let them remain outstanding with the interest running thereon, and "payable" when they are fully matured and payable on presentation at the Treasury, at which time they cease to bear interest. Some bonds are redeemable at the pleasure of the Government after a date fixed Distinction between "redeemable" and "payable."

therein, and some between certain stated times at the expiration of which they become payable, and others are payable at a fixed day certain, as stated in the account of the several outstanding loans in *Chapter I.*

Payment of matured bonds.

When the principal of any bonds becomes payable, either by maturity of the bonds or by reason of their being called in for redemption, they are paid only by the Treasurer of the United States at Washington, to whom they must be forwarded, and who pays the same in coin or in coin checks on the Assistant Treasurer at New York city, as the parties presenting the bonds desire.

Calling in 5-20 bonds for redemption.

The act of July 14, 1870, chapter 256, for refunding the national debt, makes the following provisions for calling in the five-twenty bonds for redemption:

SEC. 4. *And be it further enacted*, That the Secretary of the Treasury is hereby authorized, with any coin in the Treasury of the United States which he may lawfully apply to such purpose, or which may be derived from the sale of any of the bonds, the issue of which is provided for in this act, to pay at par and cancel any six per cent. bonds of the United States of the kind known as five-twenty bonds, which have become or shall hereafter become redeemable by the terms of their issue.

But the particular bonds so to be paid and canceled shall in all cases be indicated and specified by class, date, and number, in the order of their numbers and issues, beginning with the first numbered and issued, in public notice to be given by the Secretary of the Treasury, and in three months after the date of such public notice the interest on the bonds so selected and advertised to be paid shall cease.

Payment of fractions of coupons on called bonds.

By the first three calls under this law the three months notice fixed for redemption of the bonds expired before the coupons thereon for the current six months became payable, so that to each bond there was one coupon upon which only a fraction of the nominal amount was due. These coupons are often detached by the holders of the bonds and purchased by dealers at their face value without either party noticing the fact of the bonds being called in for redemption.

This must occur in like manner in future calls, and in order to prevent persons from being defrauded by such errors, and to save the rights and equities of all parties buying and selling coupons, the Secretary of the Treasury has made the following regulations:

When coupons, detached from bonds that have been called in for redemption, are presented for payment, the Department will pay such portion of the interest specified in such coupons as had accrued at the day fixed in the call for the redemption of the bonds, and no more, unless the party presenting them claims payment of their nominal value, in which case the Department will retain the coupons until the bonds from which they were detached shall have been presented, and the conflicting claims adjusted.

When a called bond is presented for redemption, from which a coupon, maturing after the day fixed in the call for such redemption, shall have been detached, the nominal value of such coupon shall be deducted from the sum due upon the bond, unless the coupon shall have been paid as above; the sum thus deducted to be retained to await the presentation of the coupon and a settlement.

Calling in and payment of bonds of Funded Loan to begin with bonds last issued.

The bonds of the Funded Loan, all of which are redeemable at the pleasure of the United States after a fixed time, when called in for payment, are required by law to be called in reverse order to the five-twenty bonds; that is, beginning with those *last* issued and numbered, so that the bond first issued will be last paid. In other respects the same rules apply alike to each class of bonds. For the law *see page* 9.

## 4.

## MONTHLY DEBT STATEMENT.

Contents of monthly debt statement.

On the first day of each month the Secretary of the Treasury publishes a complete, carefully prepared, and thoroughly accurate statement of the whole public debt, as it appears upon the books of the Department on that day, setting forth—

*First*. DEBT BEARING INTEREST IN COIN, under which is given the title of each outstanding loan not matured, dates of acts of authorization, rate of interest, when the principal is redeemable and payable, times of payment of interest, amount of registered bonds, amount of coupon bonds, total, interest due and unpaid, and accrued interest.

*Second.* DEBT BEARING INTEREST IN LAWFUL MONEY, including the three per cent. certificates, navy pension fund, and certificates of indebtedness of 1870.

*Third.* DEBT ON WHICH INTEREST HAS CEASED SINCE MATURITY. Under this head are included the balances of all loans matured or called in for redemption and not presented for payment, specifying each by the title of the loan, except those matured prior to 1837, which are combined in one item.

*Fourth.* DEBT BEARING NO INTEREST, giving the amount of United States notes, fractional currency, coin certificates, certificates of deposit, and unclaimed interest.

To which is added a RECAPITULATION, with a statement of the amount of coin and currency in the Treasury, the amount of reduction of the debt during the preceding month and other periods of time, and an account of BONDS ISSUED TO THE PACIFIC RAILWAY COMPANIES.

Circulation of monthly debt statement.

This monthly debt statement is printed on sheets and forwarded by mail to all journalists, bankers, brokers, and other persons in this country and Europe who request copies, or who are known to desire them, as well as to Government officials at home and abroad, for distribution, and is so extensively circulated throughout the United States that every citizen may easily know each month the exact condition of the national debt.

# CHAPTER VI.

## OBLIGATION TO PAY PRINCIPAL AND INTEREST IN COIN; SINKING FUND AND TAXATION OF BONDS.



### 1.

### PAYMENT IN COIN.

Terms of the bonds.

All the bonds of the United States, both coupon and registered, of loans mentioned in Chapter I, as well as of other loans heretofore paid in coin, express on the face thereof the promise of the Government to pay a certain amount of *dollars* with interest at the rate stated, without in any case specifying what kind of dollars are intended thereby, or in what money, whether coin or currency, either the principal or interest is payable.

Loans before February 25, 1862.

Of the loans created before the passage of the act of February 25, 1862, chapter 33, which first authorized the issue of legal-tender notes, payment could never have been contemplated at the time of negotiation in any dollars other than coin, as none other then formed the currency of the country which public or private creditors were obliged to accept. The language of the Supreme Court of the United States, in *Bank* v. *Supervisors*, (7 *Wallace*, 26,) is as applicable to these bonds as to the notes to which it refers:

"Every one of them expresses upon its face an engagement of the nation to pay to the bearer a certain sum. The dollar note is an engagement to pay *a dollar*, and the dollar intended is the coined dollar of the United States; a certain quantity in weight and fineness of gold or silver, authenticated as such by the stamp of the Government. No other dollars had before been recognized by the legislation of the national Government as lawful money."

Under the act of February 25, 1862.

The act of February 25, 1862, section 1, authorizing the issue of United States notes, provided that they should be receivable in payment of "all claims and demands against the United States of every kind whatsoever except for interest upon bonds and notes, which shall be paid in coin;" and that they should be "lawful money and a legal tender in payment of all debts, public and private, within the United States, except duties on imports and interest as aforesaid."

The subsequent laws, increasing the issue of notes and making them in like manner a legal tender, contain the same exceptions.

The same act, by section 2, authorized the issue of five hundred millions dollars of bonds, "Five-twenties of 1862," and, by section 5 enacted, that the duties on imports should be paid in coin, part of which should be set aside as a special fund, to pay in coin the interest on the bonds and notes of the United States and to establish a sinking-fund for the purchase or payment of the public debt.

—under other acts.

The act of March 3, 1863, chapter 73, authorizing the loan of that date, expressly provided that the principal and interest of the bonds issued thereunder should be payable in coin; and so did the act of March 3, 1864, chapter 17, under which the "Ten-forty" loan and the "Five-twenty loan of March, 1864," were issued.

The act of June 30, 1864, chapter 172, which authorized the "Five-twenty loan of June, 1864," provided that the *interest* should be payable in coin, without any mention of what kind of money the principal should be payable in. The act of March 3, 1865, chapter 77, under which were issued the "Five-twenties of 1865" and all the "Consols of 1865, 1867, and 1868," authorizing the issue of both bonds and treasury notes, provided that the "principal or interest, or both, may be made payable in coin or in lawful money;" "that the rate of interest on any such bonds or treasury notes, when payable in coin, shall not exceed six per centum per annum; and when payable in currency shall not exceed $7\frac{3}{10}$ per centum per annum, and the rate and character of interest shall be expressed on all such bonds or treasury notes." The *bonds* issued by authority of each of these acts were made payable *in dollars*, both principal and interest, without specifying coin or currency, while the treasury notes were invariably made payable on the face thereof in currency or lawful money.

Contemporaneous construction.

Thus the construction of the Treasury Department, contemporaneous with the issue of the bonds, seems to have been that, when not otherwise expressly provided in the bonds themselves, both the principal and interest were payable in coin; and this construction has been strictly followed and maintained by the Government by the prompt and faithful payment of every such bond in coin at maturity. And the question has been further settled by legislation, so far as subsequent legislation can affect it, by the passage of a law, which was the first act of a general nature signed by President Grant upon his accession to the Presidency, only fourteen days after his inauguration, and was an emphatic expression of the sentiment of the people of the country, uttered by a new Congress then recently elected and just commencing its first session. The following is a copy of the law:

ACT OF 1869, CHAPTER 1.

AN ACT TO STRENGTHEN THE PUBLIC CREDIT.

Act to strengthen the public credit.

*Be it enacted by the Senate and House of Representatives of the United States of America in Congress assembled*, That in order to remove any doubt as to the purpose of the Government to discharge all just obligations to the public creditors, and to settle conflicting questions and interpretations of the laws by virtue of which such obligations have been contracted, it is hereby provided and declared that the faith of the United States is solemnly pledged to the payment in coin or its equivalent of all the obligations of the United States not bearing interest, known as United States notes, and of all the interest-bearing obligations of the United States, except in cases where the law authorizing the issue of any such obligation has expressly provided that the same may be paid in lawful money or other currency than gold and silver. But none of said interest-bearing obligations not already due shall be redeemed or paid before maturity unless at such time United States notes shall be convertible into coin at the option of the holder, or unless at such time

6

bonds of the United States bearing a lower rate of interest than the bonds to be redeemed can be sold at par in coin.

And the United States also solemnly pledges its faith to make provision at the earliest practicable period for the redemption of the United States notes in coin.

J. G. BLAINE,
*Speaker of the House of Representatives.*
SCHUYLER COLFAX,
*Vice President of the United States and President of the Senate.*

*Approved March* 18, 1869.
U. S. GRANT.

Funded Loan expressly payable in coin.

To avoid all possible question as to the meaning of the dollars mentioned in the "Funded Loan," the act of July 14, 1870, which authorized its issue, expressly provides that the bonds shall be redeemable *in coin at its then standard value;* that the interest shall be payable *in such coin,* and that those conditions shall be set forth and expressed upon the face of the bonds. The obligation to pay in coin of a fixed standard value, being thus expressed in the law and in all the bonds themselves, enters into and forms part of the original contract with the holders of these securities, and can never be questioned.

## 2.

## SINKING FUND.

Law of Congress.

This fund is required to be maintained by the following provisions of the act of February 25, 1862:

SEC. 5. *And be it further enacted,* That all duties on imported goods shall be paid in coin, or in notes payable on demand heretofore authorized to be issued and by law receivable in payment of public dues, and the coin so paid shall be set apart as a special fund, and shall be applied as follows:

First. To the payment in coin of the interest on the bonds and notes of the United States.

Second. To the purchase or payment of one per centum of the entire debt of the United States, to be made within each fiscal year after the first day of July, eighteen hundred and sixty-two, which is to be set apart as a sinking fund, and the interest of which shall in like manner be applied to the purchase or payment of the public debt as the Secretary of the Treasury shall from time to time direct.

Third. The residue thereof to be paid into the Treasury of the United States.

Congress, by joint resolution of March 17, 1864, chapter 20, gave the Secretary of the Treasury permission to sell gold in the Treasury, but added a proviso that the obligation to create the sinking fund, according to the act of February 25, 1862, should not be impaired.

Fund not commenced during the war.

During the continuance of the war of the Rebellion, while the Government was still borrowing money, and was paying old loans and creating new ones, no steps were taken to establish the sinking fund as such, but the coin in the Treasury was allowed to accumulate to about one hundred millions of dollars.

First put in operation in 1869.

Upon the coming in of the administration of President Grant, in March, 1869, his Secretary of the Treasury, Hon. George S. Boutwell, immediately commenced the sinking fund, in literal compliance with the law of Congress.

Within each fiscal year, which ends June 30, the Secretary applies coin received from duties to the purchase of bonds to the amount of one per cent. of the entire debt of the United States.

The bonds so purchased were at first all registered in the name of the Treasurer of the United States, in trust for the Government, and were stamped with the words "Sinking Fund" on the face of each bond. The interest thereon was regularly collected in coin semi-annually and applied to the purchase of other bonds, which in like manner were added to the same fund.

Bonds purchased are canceled.

By section 6 of the refunding act of July 14, 1870, which is as follows, Congress required the bonds to be canceled:

SEC. 6. *And be it further enacted*, That the United States bonds purchased and now held in the Treasury in accordance with the provisions, relating to a sinking fund, of section five of the act entitled "An act to authorize the issue of United States notes, and for the redemption or funding thereof, and for funding the floating debt of the United States," approved February twenty-fifth, eighteen hundred and sixty-two, and all other United States bonds which have been purchased by the Secretary of the Treasury with surplus funds in the Treasury, and now held in the Treasury of the United States, shall be canceled and destroyed, a detailed record of such bonds so canceled and destroyed to be first made in the books of the Treasury Department.

Any bonds hereafter applied to said sinking fund, and all other United States bonds redeemed or paid hereafter by the United States, shall also in like manner be recorded, canceled, and destroyed, and the amount of the bonds of each class that have been canceled and destroyed shall be deducted respectively from the amount of each class of the outstanding debt of the United States.

In addition to other amounts that may be applied to the redemption or payment of the public debt, an amount equal to the interest on all bonds belonging to the aforesaid sinking fund shall be applied, as the Secretary of the Treasury shall from time to time direct, to the payment of the public debt, as provided for in section five of the act aforesaid. And the amount so to be applied is hereby appropriated annually for that purpose out of the receipts for duties on imported goods.

This was not an abandonment of the sinking fund, but only a different method of procedure in relation to it.

Under the requirements of this act, all bonds purchased for this fund are canceled and destroyed, but an accurate account is kept thereof, and of all subsequent purchases for the same purpose, and of the semi-annual interest on the whole, as though the bonds were in existence.

Fund, how managed.

Within each fiscal year coin received from duties to the amount of one per cent. of the entire debt of every kind, including bonds, notes, and all other obligations, and also coin equal to the amount of the interest on all the bonds previously purchased for the same purpose and canceled, is applied to the purchase of outstanding bonds, and although the bonds themselves, the mere evidences of indebtedness, are destroyed, the amount thereof is carried to the account of the sinking fund, which is thus kept up and treated as a solemn obligation of the Government. The account fixes and determines the amount of coin equal to that which would be the interest on all the bonds purchased therefor, and which must be by law, and, in fact, is semi-annually applied to the purchase of other bonds for the same account, in addition to the amount of one per cent. of the entire debt.

There have never been any trustees, managers, or commissioners of this fund, the whole business being done in the Treasury Department, under the direction of the Secretary of the Treasury, without cost or expense of any kind to the Government. It was deemed best to cancel and destroy the bonds themselves, rather than keep them in existence in the custody of the Treasurer; the obligation of the Government to use an amount of coin equal to the interest thereon, in the purchase or payment of other bonds, being as well evidenced by the books of the Department as by printed securities, and the danger of reissue being thereby avoided.

The great revenues of the country in excess of the expenditures have enabled the Secretary to purchase bonds much more extensively than the sinking-fund law absolutely requires, and the debt has been more rapidly reduced than by the operation of that fund alone.

Will extinguish the debt in about thirty years.

But the sinking fund itself will extinguish the entire national debt in about thirty years, or soon after the close of the nineteenth century, the exact time depending upon the price at which the purchases may be made in future. If the Government should at any time be obliged to pay a large premium, as it has done heretofore to extinguish former debts, which premium in some cases has exceeded twenty per cent. in coin, the operation of the sinking fund will be somewhat less effective than it has been in the past.

The Government must, under this law, continue to be a regular purchaser of its bonds, thus making a constant, well known, and certain market for the same.

## 3.

## TAXATION OF UNITED STATES BONDS AND OTHER OBLIGATIONS.

Decisions of Supreme Court.

It was decided by the Supreme Court in the year 1829, before there were any statute provisions on the subject, in the case of *Weston* v. *The City Council of Charleston*, (2 *Peters*, 449,) that a tax by a State on United States stock is unconstitutional and void. Chief Justice Marshall, in giving the opinion of the court, says: "The tax on Government stock is thought by this court to be a tax on the contract, a tax on the power to borrow money on the credit of the United States, and consequently repugnant to the Constitution," and that principle is recognized in the case of the *Bank of Commerce* v. *New York City*, (2 *Black*, 620,) and in other cases.

Taxation of banks holding bonds.

A tax by a State on State banks, upon a valuation equal to the amount of their capital stock paid in or secured to be paid in, was decided to be a tax on the property of the institution, and where that property consists of stocks of the Federal Government the law laying the tax is held void. (*Bank of Commerce* v. *New York City*, 2 *Black*, 620; *Bank Tax Case*, 2 *Wallace*, 200, explained in *Provident Institution* v. *Massachusetts*, 6 *Wallace*, 629.)

Taxation of banks whose capital is invested in United States bonds.

But national banks may be taxed by States without regard to the fact that part of their capital is invested in United States bonds, under the provisions of the national banking law of June 3, 1864, section 41. (*See notes to that section.*)

Savings banks may be taxed on their deposits, although invested in United States securities.

A State law, taxing savings banks a percentage on the average amount of their deposits, although a portion of the same is invested in securities of the United States, is a tax on the franchise of the bank and not on its property, and so is valid. (*Society for Savings* v. *Coite*, 6 *Wallace*, 594; *Provident Institution* v. *Massachusetts*, 6 *Wallace*, 611.)

Laws expressly exempting United States obligations from taxation by State authority.

The act of February 25, 1862, chapter 33, section 2, expressly provides that "all stocks, bonds, and other securities of the United States held by individuals, corporations, or associations, within the United States, shall be exempt from taxation *by or under State authority;*" the act of June 30, 1864, chapter 172, section 1, that "all bonds, treasury notes, and other obligations of the United States shall be exempt from taxation *by or under State or municipal authority;*" and several other acts contain similar provisions.

United States notes exempt from taxation.

The Supreme Court, in the case of *Bank* v. *Supervisors*, (7 *Wallace*, 26,) decided that United States notes or legal-tender notes are obligations within the meaning of the acts exempting United States obligations from State and municipal taxation.

As to all bonds and securities of the United States, except those of the Funded Loan, the exemption is only from taxation by *State or municipal authority*, and not by the Federal Government; and the latter for many years did lay an income tax upon the interest received by its citizens on such securities, and has the right to do so again.

**United States Government may tax bonds.**

But the bonds of the Funded Loan are by the express terms of the act of July 14, 1870, and by the language of the bonds themselves, "exempt from the payment of all taxes or duties of the United States, as well as from taxation in any form, by or under State, municipal, or local authority." This exemption is as extensive as the legislative power can make it, and entering into the original contract, by being incorporated into the act under which the bonds are issued and into the language of the bonds also, secures to the holders of the bonds of this loan, unlike those of any other loan ever issued by the Government, the full amount of interest thereon, without deduction by taxation in any form whatever, either by the States or the national Government itself.

**Except those of the Funded Loan.**

# CHAPTER VII.

## ESTABLISHED POLICY OF THE COUNTRY, COEVAL WITH THE CONSTITUTION, TO MAINTAIN THE PUBLIC CREDIT, TO GRADUALLY PAY THE PRINCIPAL OF ALL LOANS, AND TO AVOID A PERMANENT NATIONAL DEBT.

1. Extinguishment of the public debt.
2–9. Extracts from messages of the Presidents.
10. The country free from public debt.
11. Premiums paid to redeem debts before maturity.
12. Reduction of the existing debt.
13. List of loans heretofore contracted.

### 1.

### EXTINGUISHMENT OF THE PUBLIC DEBT.

The policy to pay off the debt, long established.

The following extracts from the messages of Presidents of the United States, who for the time being generally represent the prevailing sentiment of the people who elect them, indicate the policy of the country adopted in the early days of the national Government, and ever since steadily pursued, for a period of nearly a century, to maintain faithfully the public credit, not only by prompt payment of the interest, but by the gradual extinguishment of the principal also of all national loans, whether contracted under ordinary or extraordinary circumstances, or for usual and permanent or temporary and special purposes.

### 2.

### WASHINGTON'S SECOND ANNUAL MESSAGE TO CONGRESS, DECEMBER 8, 1790.

Washington, 1790.

"Allow me, moreover, to hope that it will be a favorite policy with you not merely to secure a payment of the interest of the debt funded, but as far and as fast as the growing resources of the country will permit, to exonerate it of the principal itself. The appropriations you have made of the western lands explain your disposition on this subject, and I am persuaded that the sooner that valuable fund can be made to contribute, along with other means, to the actual reduction of the public debt, the more salutary will the measure be to every public interest as well as the more satisfactory to our constituents."

3.

WASHINGTON'S FOURTH ANNUAL MESSAGE, NOVEMBER 6, 1792.

"I entertain a strong hope that the state of the national finances is now sufficiently matured to enable you to enter upon a systematic and effectual arrangement for the regular redemption and discharge of the public debt, according to the right which has been reserved to the Government. No measure can be more desirable, whether viewed with an eye to its intrinsic importance, or to the general sentiment and wish of the nation." Washington, 1792.

4.

WASHINGTON'S SIXTH ANNUAL MESSAGE, 1794.

"The time which has elapsed since the commencement of our fiscal measures, has developed our pecuniary resources so as to open the way for a definitive plan for the redemption of the public debt. It is believed that the result is such as to encourage Congress to consummate this work without delay. Nothing can more promote the permanent welfare of the nation, and nothing would be more grateful to our constituents. Indeed, whatever is unfinished of our system of public credit, cannot be benefited by procrastination; and, as far as may be practicable, we ought to place that credit on grounds which cannot be disturbed, and to prevent that progressive accumulation of debt which must ultimately endanger all governments." Washington, 1794

5.

WASHINGTON'S SEVENTH ANNUAL MESSAGE, 1795.

"Whether measures may not be advisable to reinforce the provision for the redemption of the public debt, will naturally engage your examination. Congress have demonstrated their sense to be, and it were superfluous to repeat mine, that whatsoever will tend to accelerate the honorable extinc- Washington, 1795.

tion of our public debt accords as much with the true interests of our country as with the general sense of our constituents."

6.

WASHINGTON'S EIGHTH ANNUAL MESSAGE, 1796.

Washington, 1796. "A reinforcement of the existing provisions for discharging our public debt was mentioned in my address at the opening of the last session. Some preliminary steps were taken toward it, the maturing of which will, no doubt, engage your zealous attention during the present session. I will only add, that it will afford me a heartfelt satisfaction to concur in such further measures as will ascertain to our country the prospect of a speedy extinguishment of the debt. Posterity may have cause to regret if from any motive intervals of tranquillity are left unimproved for accelerating this valuable end."

7.

WASHINGTON'S FAREWELL ADDRESS.

Washington, 1796. "As a very important source of strength and security, cherish public credit. One method of preserving it is to use it as sparingly as possible, avoiding occasions of expense by cultivating peace, but remembering, also, that timely disbursements to prepare for danger frequently prevent much greater disbursements to repel it; avoiding likewise the accumulation of debt, not only by shunning occasions of expense, but by vigorous exertions in time of peace to discharge the debts which unavoidable wars have occasioned, not ungenerously throwing upon posterity the burden which we ourselves ought to bear."

8.

PRESIDENT JOHN ADAMS'S FIRST ANNUAL MESSAGE, 1797.

President John Adams, 1797. "Since the decay of the feudal system, by which the public defense was provided for chiefly at the expense of individuals, the system of loans has been introduced; and as no nation can raise within the year by taxes sufficient sums for defense and for military operations in time of war, the sums loaned and debts contracted have necessarily become the subjects of what have been called funding systems.

The consequences arising from the continued accumulation of public debts in other countries, ought to admonish us to be careful to prevent their growth in our own case. The national defense must be provided for as well as the support of Government, but both should be accomplished as much as possible by immediate taxes, and as little as possible by loans."

9.

PRESIDENT JOHN QUINCY ADAMS'S THIRD ANNUAL MESSAGE, 1827.

"The deep solicitude felt by our citizens of all classes throughout the Union for the total discharge of the public debt, will apologize for the earnestness with which I deem it my duty to urge this topic upon the consideration of Congress—of recommending to them again the observance of the strictest economy in the public funds."

President J. Q. Adams, 1827.

10.

THE COUNTRY FREE FROM PUBLIC DEBT.

"President Jackson, in his seventh annual message to Congress, December, 1835, made the following announcement: 'Since my last annual communication all the remains of the public debt have been redeemed, or money has been placed in deposit for this purpose, whenever the creditors choose to receive it. All the other pecuniary engagements of the Government have been honorably and promptly fulfilled, and there will be a balance in the Treasury at the close of the present year of about nineteen millions of dollars."

President Jackson, 1835.

The country free from debt.

In 1834 and 1835 the country was entirely out of debt, and in honor of the event a celebration was had in Washington on the 8th of January, 1835, the anniversary of the battle of New Orleans, at which were present about two hundred and fifty of the representative men of the country. Andrew Jackson, then President, was not himself present, but he sent the following sentiment:

Celebration of the event.

"*The payment of the Public Debt:* Let us commemorate it as an event which gives us increased power as a nation and reflects lustre on our Federal Union, of whose justice, fidelity, and wisdom, it is a glorious illustration."

James K. Polk, afterwards President of the United States, then first vice president of the occasion, in his remarks, said: "The day of the final payment of the national debt *must* be a day of national rejoicing. The only national debt that now remains is that debt of gratitude we owe to those who established and those who sustained our national freedom. We hail the extinguishment, at so early a period, of the public debt created by two wars, the one to purchase, the other to preserve and protect public liberty, as the result of a wise, economical, and patriotic administration of public affairs."

Surplus revenue distributed to the States.

On the first day of January, 1837, there was in the Treasury a balance of $37,327,252 69; and of that amount, by an act of Congress passed June, 1836, the sum of $28,101,644 91 was apportioned to and actually distributed among the several States.

### 11.

### Premiums Paid to Redeem Debts before Maturity.

Premiums paid for bonds.

On several occasions the Government has purchased its outstanding debts before maturity at large premiums in in coin. In 1842 at an average premium of $15\frac{75}{100}$ per cent.; in 1846 at $7\frac{35}{100}$ per cent.; in 1847 at $20\frac{94}{100}$ per cent.; and in 1848 at $20\frac{95}{100}$ average. In some cases bonds were purchased at a premium as high as 23 per cent. in coin.

### 12.

### Reduction of the Existing Debt.

Reduction of existing debt.

The public debt, as represented on the books of the Treasury Department, exclusive of Pacific Railway bonds and of accrued interest, (which until 1869 was not included in the debt statement,) and deducting therefrom the cash in the Treasury, reached its highest point March 1, 1866, when it stood at $2,707,856,000 22.

Immediately after the close of the Rebellion it was reduced by the proceeds of the sale of materials of war; and since then it has been further reduced by the surplus revenue of the Government until, on the first of September, 1872, it stood, including accrued interest and interest due and unpaid, less cash in the Treasury, at $2,177,322,020 55; showing a reduction in five and a half years of $564,599,335 35.

By the operation of the Sinking Fund, the debt must continue to be reduced annually till it is finally extinguished. *See page* 82.

President Grant, in his inaugural address, March 4, 1869, said, in relation to the debt:

"A great debt has been contracted in securing to us and to our posterity the Union. The payment of this, *principal* and *interest*, as well as the return to a specie basis as soon as it can be accomplished without material detriment to the debtor class or to the country at large, must be provided for. To protect the national honor, every dollar of Government indebtedness should be paid in gold, unless otherwise stipulated in the contract."

13.

## LIST OF ALL LOANS HERETOFORE CONTRACTED.

There can be no better evidence of the policy of the country than the following complete list of all debts which have been contracted by the Government from 1776 to the present time, all of which have been fully paid and canceled or called in for payment, except so much as remains of those incurred since 1858, contracted mostly on account of the Rebellion, and which have been rapidly reduced since the establishment of peace, as fully set forth in the foregoing pages: List of all loans

| Title of Loan. | Act of authorization. | Amount issued. |
|---|---|---|
| Farmers General of France | December 23, 1776 | $181,500 00 |
| Loan of 18 million livres, France | December 23, 1776, December 3, 1777 | 3,267,000 00 |
| " 1781 from Spain | September 28, 1779 | 174,017 13 |
| " 10 million livres from France | October 26, 1779 | 1,815,000 00 |
| " 6 " " " | " " | 1,089,000 00 |
| Balance of supplies due France | " " | 24,332 86 |
| Loan of 1782, Holland | " " | 2,000,000 00 |

| Title of Loan. | Act of authorization. | Amount issued. |
|---|---|---|
| Loan of 1784, Holland | October 27, 1779 | 800,000 00 |
| " 1787 " | " " | 400,000 00 |
| " 1788 " | " " | 400,000 00 |
| " 1790 " | August 4 and 12, 1790. | 1,200,000 00 |
| " March, 1791, Holland | " " " | 1,000,000 00 |
| " September, 1791 " | " " " | 2,400,000 00 |
| " November, 1791, Antwerp | " " " | 820,000 00 |
| " December, 1791, Holland | " " " | 1,200,000 00 |
| " 1792 " | " " " | 1,180,000 00 |
| " 1793 " | " " " | 400,000 00 |
| " 1794 " | " " " | 1,200,000 00 |
| Debts due foreign officers | May 8, 1792 | 186,988 78 |
| Debts due from old government | | 502,465 32 |
| Temporary loans of 1789 and 1790 | | 246,608 81 |
| Six per cent. stock of 1790 | August 4 and 12, 1790. | 29,507,522 78 |
| Deferred six per cent. stock | " " " | 14,622,600 98 |
| Three per cent. stock | " " " | 19,094,231 62 |
| Subscription loan of 1791, B. U. S. | February 25, 1791 | 2,000,000 00 |
| Temporary loan, B'k of N. America | March 3, 1791 | 156,595 56 |
| " " 1792, B. U. S. | May 2, 1792 | 400,000 00 |
| " " 1793 " | February 28, 1793. | 800,000 00 |
| " " 1794, B'k of N. Y. | March 20, 1794 | 200,000 00 |
| " " March, 1794, B. U. S. | " " | 1,000,000 00 |
| " " June " " | June 9, 1794 | 1,000,000 00 |
| " " Dec. " " | December 18, 1794 | 2,000,000 00 |
| " " Feb., 1795 " | February 21, 1795 | 800,000 00 |
| " " March A " " | March 3, 1795 | 500,000 00 |
| " " " B " " | " " | 500,000 00 |
| " " " C " " | " " | 500,000 00 |
| Five and ½ per cent. stock of 1795 | " " | 1,848,900 00 |
| Four and ½ per cent. stock of " | " " | 176,000 00 |
| Temporary loan, Bank of New York | May 31, 1796 | 320,000 00 |
| " " 1798, B. U. S. | March 3, 1795 | 200,000 00 |
| Six per cent. stock of 1796 | May 31, 1796 | 80,000 00 |
| Navy six per cent. stock | June 30, 1798 | 711,700 00 |
| Eight per cent. stock of 1798 | July 16, 1798 | 5,000,000 00 |
| Eight per cent. stock of 1800 | May 7, 1800 | 1,481,700 00 |
| Louisiana six per cent. stock | November 10, 1803 | 11,250,000 00 |
| Exchanged six per cent. stock of 1807 | February 11, 1807 | 6,294,051 12 |
| Converted " " " " | " " | 1,859 850 70 |
| Temporary loan of 1810 | May 1, 1810 | 2,750,000 00 |
| Six per cent. stock of 1812 | March 14, 1812 | 8,134,700 00 |
| Temporary loan of 1812 | " " | 2,150,000 00 |
| Treasury notes of 1812 | June 30, 1812 | 5,000,000 00 |
| Exchanged six per cent. stock of 1812 | July 6, 1812 | 2,984,746 72 |
| Six per cent. loan of February, 1813 | February 8, 1813 | 18,109,377 43 |
| Treasury notes of 1813 | February 25, 1813 | 5,000,000 00 |
| Six per cent. loan of August, 1813 | August 2, 1813 | 8,498,581 95 |
| Treasury notes of March, 1814 | March 4, 1814 | 10,000,000 00 |
| Ten million loan of 1814 | March 24, 1814 | 9,919,476 25 |
| Six " " " | " " | 5,384,134 87 |
| Undesignated six per cent. stock of 1814 | " " | 746,403 31 |
| Mississippi stock | March 31, 1814 | 4,282,151 12 |
| Temporary loan of 1814 | November 15, 1814 | 1,450,000 00 |
| Treasury notes, December, 1814 | December 26, 1814 | 8,318,400 00 |
| Direct tax loan | January 9, 1815 | 200,000 00 |

| Title of Loan. | Date of authorization. | Amount issued. |
|---|---|---|
| Temporary loan, February, 1815...... | February 13, 1815..... | $225,000 00 |
| Seven per cent. stock of 1815.......... | February 24, 1815..... | 9,070,386 00 |
| Treasury notes of 1815................. | February 24, 1815..... | 4,969,400 00 |
| Small treasury notes..................... | ...... "..........."......... | 3,392,994 00 |
| Treasury note six per cent. stock...... | ...... "..........."......... | 1,505,352 18 |
| Temporary loan March, 1815.......... | March 3, 1815.......... | 1,150,000 00 |
| Six per cent. stock of 1815.............. | ...... "......"............... | 12,288,147 56 |
| Subscription loan to Bank U. S....... | April 10, 1816......... | 7,000,000 00 |
| Five per cent. stock of 1820............ | May 15, 1820........... | 999,999 13 |
| Six......"........."........"............ | "......."................. | 2,000,000 00 |
| Five....."........."........1821............ | March 3, 1821.......... | 4,735,296 30 |
| Exchanged five per cent. of 1822...... | April 20, 1822......... | 56,704 77 |
| Four and ½ per cent. stock May 24, '24.. | May 24, 1824........... | 5,000,000 00 |
| Exchanged four and ½ per cent. stock.. | May 26, 1824........... | 4,454,727 95 |
| Four and ½ per cent. stock May 26, '24. | "......."................. | 5,000,000 00 |
| Exchanged four and ½ per ct. stock 1825.............................. | March 3, 1825......... | 1,539,336 16 |
| Treasury notes of 1837................. | October 12, 1837...... | 10,000,000 00 |
| " " 1838................. | May 21, 1838........... | 5,709,810 01 |
| " " 1839................. | March 2, 1839......... | 3,857,276 21 |
| " " 1840................. | ".....31, 1840......... | 7,114,251 31 |
| " " 1841................. | February 15, 1841..... | 7,529,062 75 |
| Loan of 1841............................ | July 21, 1841.. ........ | 5,672,976 88 |
| Treasury notes of January, 1842...... | January 31, 1842...... | 7,959,994 83 |
| Loan of 1842............................ | July 21, 1841, April 15, 1842............ | 8,000,000 00 |
| Treasury notes of August, 1842....... | August 31, 1842....... | 3,025,554 89 |
| " " " 1843....... | March 3, 1843.......... | 1,806,950 00 |
| Loan of 1843.............................. | "......."................. | 7,004,231 35 |
| Treasury notes of January, 1846...... | January 28, 1846...... | 26,122,100 00 |
| " " July, 1846........... | July 22, 1846........... | 7,687,800 00 |
| Loan of 1846.............................. | "......"................. | 4,999,149 45 |
| Mexican indemnity stock............... | August 10, 1846........ | 303,573 92 |
| Loan of 1847.............................. | January 28, 1847...... | 28,207,000 00 |
| Bounty land scrip........................ | February 11, 1847..... | 233,075 00 |
| Loan of 1848.............................. | March 31, 1848......... | 16,000,000 00 |
| Texan indemnity stock.................. | September 9, 1850..... | 5,000,000 00 |
| Treasury notes of 1857................ | December 23, 1857.... | 20,000,000 00 |
| Loan of 1858.............................. | June 14, 1858.......... | 20,000,000 00 |
| Loan of 1860.............................. | June 22, 1860.......... | 7,022,000 00 |
| Treasury notes of 1860................. | December 17, 1860.... | 10,010,900 00 |
| Loan of February, 1861, (81's)......... | February 8, 1861...... | 18,415,000 00 |
| Treasury notes of 1861................. | ....."........."........... | |
| " " "......................... | June 22, 1860.......... | |
| " " "......................... | March 2, 1861.......... | |
| Sixty days Treasury notes.............. | "......"............... | 35,409,350 00 |
| Oregon war debt.......................... | "......"............... | 1,090,850 00 |
| Old demand notes....................... | July 17, Aug. 5, '61, and Feb. 12, 1862 | 60,000,000 00 |
| Loan of July and August, 1861, (81's). | ..............."............. | 189,318,100 00 |
| Seven-thirties of 1861.................. | ..............."............. | 140,094,750 00 |
| Subscription loan, Nov. 16, 1861...... | ..............."............. | 46,303,129 17 |
| Five-twenties of 1862................... | February 25, 1862.... | 514,771,600 00 |
| United States notes..................... | Feb. 25, July 11, '62 March 3, 1863.... | 432,757,601 00 |
| Temporary loan........................ | Feb. 25, Mar. 17, '62 June 30, 1864..... | 131,497,853 62 |

| Title of Loan. | Date of authorization. | Amount issued. |
|---|---|---|
| Certificates of indebtedness.......... | Mar. 1 and 17, 1862, and March 3, '63. | 236,373,000 00 |
| Fractional currency.................. | July 17, '62, Mar. 3, '63, June 30, '64. | 43,179,650 03 |
| Loan of 1863, (81's)...................... | March 3, 1863......... | 75,000,000 00 |
| One-year notes of 1863................ | "......."............... | 44,520,000 00 |
| Two " " ................ | "..... ."............... | 166,480,000 00 |
| Compound interest notes............... | Mar. 3,'63, June 30,'64 | 217,024,160 00 |
| Coin certificates......................... | "....." (§ 5)............ | 50,392,180 00 |
| Ten-forties of 1864...... ................ | ".....1864............... | 196,117,300 00 |
| Five-twenties of March, 1864......... | "......."................ | 3,882,500 00 |
| " June, 1864......... | June 30, 1864......... | 125,561,300 00 |
| Seven-thirties of 1864–1865..... ... | June 30, 1864, Mar. 3, 1865............ | 830,000,000 00 |
| Five-twenties '65, consols '65, '7, '8... | ........."................. | 958,467,900 00 |
| Three per cent. certificates............ | March 2, 1867......... | 65,230,000 00 |
| Certificates of indebtedness, 1870...... | July 8, 1870........... | 678,362 41 |
| Funded loan of 1881..................... | July 14, 1870.......... | 200,000,000 00 |

In the foregoing list the amount set down to each of those items of indebtedness in which the certificates, notes, or currency were issued and reissued, is the largest amount outstanding at any one time.

# PART II.

THE NATIONAL BANKING LAWS OF THE UNITED STATES, WITH NOTES AND REFERENCES TO THE DECISIONS OF THE COURTS AND OPINIONS OF THE ATTORNEYS GENERAL THEREON.

# INTRODUCTORY OBSERVATIONS.

---

The necessities of the Government, created by the great Rebellion, brought into operation many powers conferred upon Congress by the Constitution, which until that time had rarely or never been exercised, and new and extraordinary legislation relating to the finances and financial condition of the country was enacted in order to supply the wants of the national Government.

Previously to the year 1863 Congress had never interfered with the banks of issue created by the several States, except in 1813 to levy, temporarily, a small stamp tax on the notes of banks and bankers for the purpose of revenue, and in 1862 to prohibit all corporations and individuals from issuing notes of a fractional part of a dollar.

In 1836 an act was passed providing that State banks conveniently located might be selected as depositories of public money, upon certain conditions therein prescribed: one of which was, that no bank so selected should issue bills of less denomination than five dollars. The "independent treasury system," established by the acts of July 4, 1840, and August 6, 1846, superseded the employment of State banks as depositories.

At the time of the adoption of the Constitution of the United States four State banks were in existence, one in each of the States of Maryland, Massachusetts, New York, and Pennsylvania, and the number went on increasing, until, in the year 1863, there were more than one thousand five hundred in the different States, each subject to the laws of the State by which it was incorporated, but substantially independent of any legislation of Congress.

Congress twice chartered a bank of the United States, first in 1791 and again in 1816, but when the charter expired in 1836 it was not renewed, and Congress never afterwards enacted a law for the incorporation of banks, except some local banks in the District of Columbia, over which it has exclusive jurisdiction, until the passage of the act of February 25, 1863, entitled "An act to provide a national currency secured by a pledge of United States stocks, and to provide for the circulation and redemption thereof."

In order to introduce some changes in the law this act was the next year repealed, and a substitute enacted June 3, 1864, entitled "An act to provide a national currency secured by a pledge of United States bonds, and to provide for the circulation and redemption thereof;" which, with the amendments thereto, is printed in the following pages.

Under the operation of these laws and the 9th section of the act of July 13, 1866, and the 2d section of the act of March 26, 1867, taxing the notes of State banks and of towns, cities, municipal corporations, and individuals, used for circulation, nearly all the State banks have been converted into national banks or gone out of existence, and those few which remain have ceased to issue notes for circulation, finding it unprofitable to do so.

All paper money has disappeared from circulation, except United States legal-tender notes and national bank notes.

The number of national banks is now a little more than one thousand nine hundred, issuing their notes to the amount of about three hundred and forty millions of dollars.

# ACTS OF CONGRESS.

---

### ACT OF JUNE 3, 1864, CHAPTER 106.

AN ACT TO PROVIDE A NATIONAL CURRENCY SECURED BY A PLEDGE OF UNITED STATES BONDS, AND TO PROVIDE FOR THE CIRCULATION AND REDEMPTION THEREOF.

#### CURRENCY BUREAU.

Currency Bureau.

*Be it enacted by the Senate and House of Representatives of the United States of America in Congress assembled,* That there shall be established in the Treasury Department a separate bureau, which shall be charged with the execution of this and all other laws that may be passed by Congress respecting the issue and regulation of a national currency secured by United States bonds.

Comptroller of Currency.

The chief officer of the said bureau shall be denominated the Comptroller of the Currency, and shall be under the general direction of the Secretary of the Treasury. He shall be appointed by the President, on the recommendation of the Secretary of the Treasury, by and with the advice and consent of the Senate, and shall hold his office for the term of five years unless sooner removed by the President, upon reasons to be communicated by him to the Senate; he shall receive an annual salary of five thousand dollars;

Deputy Comptroller.

He shall have a competent deputy, appointed by the Secretary, whose salary shall be two thousand five hundred dollars, and who shall possess the power and perform the duties attached by law to the office of Comptroller during a vacancy in such office and during his absence or inability.

Clerks.

He shall employ, from time to time, the necessary clerks to discharge such duties as he shall direct, which clerks shall be appointed and classified by the Secretary of the Treasury in the manner now provided by law.

Oath and bond of Comptroller.

Within fifteen days from the time of notice of his appointment the Comptroller shall take and subscribe the oath of office prescribed by the Constitution and laws of the United States; and he shall give to the United States a bond in the penalty of one hundred thousand dollars, with not less than two responsible sureties, to be approved by the Secretary of the Treasury, conditioned for the faithful discharge of the duties of his office.

—of Deputy Comptroller.

The Deputy Comptroller so appointed shall also take the oath of office prescribed by the Constitution and laws of the United States, and shall give a like bond in the penalty of fifty thousand dollars.

Neither to be interested in banks.

The Comptroller and Deputy Comptroller shall not, either directly or indirectly, be interested in any association issuing national currency under the provisions of this act.

Seal of office, its use, &c.

SEC. 2. *And be it further enacted,* That the Comptroller of the Currency, with the approval of the Secretary of the Treasury, shall devise a seal, with suitable inscriptions, for his office, a description of which, with a certificate of approval by the Secretary of the Treasury, shall be filed in the office of the Secretary of State with an impression thereof, which shall thereupon become the seal of office of the Comptroller of the Currency, and the same may be renewed when necessary. Every certificate, assignment, and conveyance executed by the Comptroller, in pursuance of any authority conferred on him by law, and sealed with his seal of office, shall be received in evidence in all places and courts whatsoever; and all copies of papers in the office of the Comptroller, certified by him and authenticated by the said seal, shall in all cases be evidence equally and in like manner as the original. An impression of such seal directly on the paper shall be as valid as if made on wax or wafer.

Rooms for office, vaults, &c.

SEC. 3. *And be it further enacted,* That there shall be assigned to the Comptroller of the Currency by the Secretary of the Treasury suitable rooms in the Treasury Building for conducting the business of the Currency Bureau, in which shall be safe and secure fire-proof vaults, in which it shall be the duty of the Comptroller to deposit and safely keep all the plates not necessarily in the possession of engravers or printers, and other valuable things belonging to his department; and the Comptroller shall from time to time furnish the necessary furniture, stationery, fuel, lights, and other proper conveniences for the transaction of the said business.

### UNITED STATES BONDS DEFINED.

Definition of United States bonds as used in this act.

SEC. 4. *And be it further enacted*, That the term "United States bonds," as used in this act, shall be construed to mean all registered bonds now issued, or that may hereafter be issued, on the faith of the United States by the Secretary of the Treasury, in pursuance of law.

### BANKS, HOW FORMED.

Banking associations, how formed.

SEC. 5. *And be it further enacted*, That associations for carrying on the business of banking may be formed[1] by any number of persons, not less in any case than five, who shall enter into articles of association, which shall specify in general terms the object for which the association is formed, and may contain any other provisions, not inconsistent with the provisions of this act, which the association may see fit to adopt for the regulation of the business of the association and the conduct of its affairs, which said articles shall be signed by the persons uniting to form the association, and a copy of them forwarded to the Comptroller of the Currency, to be filed and preserved in his office.

Organization certificates.

SEC. 6. *And be it further enacted*, That the persons uniting to form such an association shall, under their hands, make an organization certificate, which shall specify—

First. The name assumed by such association, which name shall be subject to the approval of the Comptroller.

Second. The place where its operations of discount and

---

1. There is no limit to the aggregate amount of *capital* of banks which may be organized under this act. (*Opinions of Attorneys General, vol.* 11, *page* 334.)

Any number of banks may be organized, with any amount of capital, not less to each bank than the minimum specified in section 7. But each bank must deposit bonds with the Treasurer of the United States, as required by section 16, whether it obtains circulation or not. And the aggregate circulation of currency notes is limited to $354,000,000. (*See section* 22, *and note* 9.)

There is no limit to the aggregate circulation of gold notes. (*See Act of July* 12, 1870, *chapter* 252, *sections* 3, 4, 5.

deposit are to be carried on, designating the State, Territory, or District, and also the particular county and city, town, or village.

Third. The amount of its capital stock, and the number of shares into which the same shall be divided.

Fourth. The names and places of residence of the shareholders, and the number of shares held by each of them.

Fifth. A declaration that said certificate is made to enable such persons to avail themselves of the advantages of this act.

—to be acknowledged.

The said certificate shall be acknowledged before a judge of some court of record or a notary public,[2] and such certificate, with the acknowledgment thereof authenticated by the seal of such court or notary, shall be transmitted to the Comptroller of the Currency, who shall record and carefully preserve the same in his office.

Copies of, when evidence.

Copies of such certificate, duly certified by the Comptroller, and authenticated by his seal of office, shall be legal and sufficient evidence in all courts and places within the United States, or the jurisdiction of the Government thereof, of the existence of such association, and of every other matter or thing which could be proved by the production of the original certificate.

CAPITAL STOCK REQUIRED.

Amount of capital stock required.

SEC. 7. *And be it further enacted*, That no association shall be organized under this act, with a less capital than one hundred thousand dollars, nor in a city whose population exceeds fifty thousand persons, with a less capital than two hundred thousand dollars: *Provided*, That banks with a capital of not less than fifty thousand dollars may, with the approval of the Secretary of the Treasury, be organized in any place the population of which does not exceed six thousand inhabitants.

---

2. In an action by a national bank, in which the certificate of the Comptroller is produced authorizing the bank to commence business, it is no objection to its legal existence that the acknowledgment of the organization certificates was taken before a notary public who was one of the stockholders. That is a question for the Comptroller only. (*Thatcher* v. *The West River National Bank*, 19 *Michigan*, 196.)

CORPORATE EXISTENCE, POWERS, &C.

SEC. 8. *And be it further enacted*, That every association formed pursuant to the provisions of this act shall, from the date of the execution of its organization certificate, be a body corporate, but shall transact no business except such as may be incidental to its organization and necessarily preliminary, until authorized by the Comptroller of the Currency to commence the business of banking.

When a corporation.

Such association shall have power to adopt a corporate seal, and shall have succession by the name designated in its organization certificate, for the period of twenty years from its organization, unless sooner dissolved according to the provisions of its articles of association, or by the act of its shareholders owning two-thirds of its stock, or unless the franchise shall be forfeited by a violation of this act; by such name it may make contracts, sue and be sued,[3] complain and defend, in any court of law and equity, as fully as natural persons;

May adopt a seal and continue a corporation for twenty years.

May sue and be sued.

It may elect or appoint directors, and by its board of directors appoint a president, vice president, cashier,[4] and other officers, define their duties, require bonds of them and fix the penalty thereof, dismiss said officers, or any of them, at pleasure,[5] and appoint others to fill their places;

And exercise under this act all such incidental powers as shall be necessary to carry on the business of banking by discounting and negotiating promissory notes, drafts, bills of exchange, and other evidences of debt; by receiving deposits; by buying and selling exchange, coin, and bullion; by loaning money on personal security; by obtaining, issu-

What business may be transacted.

---

3. See section 50, and notes thereon.

4. The cashier is the financial officer, or the executive officer, through whom the whole financial operations of the bank are conducted. The directors may limit his authority as they deem proper, but this would not affect those to whom the limitations were unknown. His authority to do particular acts may be inferred from evidence as to the powers exercised by him, with the knowledge and acquiescence of the directors and the usage of other banks in the same city. (*Merchants' Bank* v. *State National Bank*, 10 *Wallace*, 604; *The Wakefield Bank* v. *Truesdall*, 55 *Barbour*, 602.)

5. The directors may remove the president even before any by-laws are adopted. (*Taylor* v. *Hutton*, 43 *Barbour*, 195.)

ing, and circulating notes according to the provisions of this act;

Transfer of stock.

And its board of directors shall also have power to define and regulate by by-laws, not inconsistent with the provisions of this act, the manner in which its stock shall be transferred,[6] its directors elected or appointed, its officers appointed, its property transferred, its general business conducted, and all the privileges granted by this act to associations organized under it shall be exercised and enjoyed;

Where to transact business.

And its usual business shall be transacted at an office or banking-house located in the place specified in its organization certificate.

DIRECTORS AND PRESIDENT.

Directors and president:

SEC. 9. *And be it further enacted,* That the affairs of every association shall be managed by not less than five directors, one of whom shall be the president. Every director shall, during his whole term of service, be a citizen of the United States; and at least three-fourths of the directors shall have resided in the State, Territory, or district in which such association is located one year next preceding their election as directors, and be residents of the same during their continuance in office.

—must each own ten shares and take official oath.

Each director shall own, in his own right, at least ten shares of the capital stock of the association of which he is a director. Each director, when appointed or elected, shall take an oath that he will, so far as the duty devolves on him, diligently and honestly administer the affairs of such association, and will not knowingly violate, or willingly permit

6. A bank whose certificates of stock declare the stockholders entitled to a certain number of shares, transferable in person or by attorney on the books of the bank, and upon a surrender of the certificates, *but not otherwise*, and which permits a stockholder to transfer his shares without a surrender of his certificates, is liable for value of the same stock to a bona fide transferee, who produces the certificates with a properly executed power of attorney to transfer. (*Bank* v. *Lanier*, 11 *Wallace*, 369.)

Banks have no valid liens on the shares of stockholders for debts due from them to the bank, even although the by-laws and the certificates of stock set forth such lien, unless the bank is authorized to make such a provision by the articles of association. (*Rosenback* v. *Salt Springs National Bank*, 35 *Barbour*, 495; *Bank* v. *Lanier*, 11 *Wallace*, 369.)

to be violated, any of the provisions of this act, and that he is the bona fide owner, in his own right, of the number of shares of stock required by this act, subscribed by him, or standing in his name on the books of the association, and that the same is not hypothecated, or in any way pledged, as security for any loan or debt; which oath, subscribed by himself, and certified by the officer before whom it is taken, shall be immediately transmitted to the Comptroller of the Currency, and by him filed and preserved in his office.

Term of office--elections.

SEC. 10. *And be it further enacted*, That the directors of any association first elected or appointed shall hold their places until their successors shall be elected and qualified. All subsequent elections shall be held annually on such day in the month of January as may be specified in the articles of association; and the directors so elected shall hold their places for one year, and until their successors are elected and qualified.

But any director ceasing to be the owner of the requisite amount of stock, or having in any other manner become disqualified, shall thereby vacate his place. Any vacancy in the board shall be filled by appointment by the remaining directors, and any director so appointed shall hold his place until the next election.

Election, when omitted at the appointed time.

If from any cause an election of directors shall not be made at the time appointed, the association shall not for that cause be dissolved, but an election may be held on any subsequent day, thirty days' notice thereof in all cases having been given in a newspaper published in the city, town, or county in which the association is located; and if no newspaper is published in such city, town, or county, such notice shall be published in a newspaper published nearest thereto. If the articles of association do not fix the day on which the election shall be held, or if the election should not be held on the day fixed, the day for the election shall be designated by the board of directors in their by-laws, or otherwise: *Provided*, That if the directors fail to fix the day, as aforesaid, shareholders representing two-thirds of the shares may.

Stockholders' votes: proxies.

SEC. 11. *And be it further enacted*, That in all elections of directors, and in deciding all questions at meetings of share-

No officer, &c., to act as proxy.

holders, each shareholder shall be entitled to one vote on each share of stock held by him. Shareholders may vote by proxies duly authorized in writing; but no officer, clerk, teller, or bookkeeper of such association shall act as proxy; and no shareholder whose liability is past due and unpaid shall be allowed to vote.

CAPITAL STOCK AND STOCKHOLDERS.

Shares personal property; transferable.

SEC. 12. *And be it further enacted,* That the capital stock of any association formed under this act shall be divided into shares of one hundred dollars each, and be deemed personal property and transferable on the books of the association in such manner as may be prescribed in the by-laws or articles of association; and every person becoming a shareholder by such transfer shall, in proportion to his shares, succeed to all the rights and liabilities of the prior holder of such shares, and no change shall be made in the articles of association by which the rights, remedies, or security of the existing creditors of the association shall be impaired.

Rights and liabilities of shareholders.

The shareholders of each association formed under the provisions of this act, and of each existing bank or banking association that may accept the provisions of this act, shall be held individually responsible, equally and ratably, and not one for another, for all contracts, debts, and engagements of such association to the extent of the amount of their stock therein at the par value thereof, in addition to that amount invested in such shares;[7] except the shareholders of any banking association now existing under State laws, having not less than five millions of dollars of capital actually paid in, and a surplus of twenty per centum on hand, both to be determined by the Comptroller of the Currency, shall be liable only to the amount invested in their shares;

---

7. The liability of stockholders is several, not joint. The limit of their liability is the par of the stock held by each one. Where the whole amount is sought to be recovered the proceeding must be at law. Where less is required the proceeding may be in equity for contribution, and all stockholders who can be reached by the process of the court may be joined in the suit; but it is no objection that there are others beyond the jurisdiction of the court, who cannot for that reason be made co-defendants. (*Kennedy* v. *Gibson et al.*, 8 *Wallace*, 498.)

and such surplus of twenty per centum shall be kept undiminished, and be in addition to the surplus provided for in this act; and if at any time there shall be a deficiency in said surplus of twenty per centum, the said banking association shall not pay any dividends to its shareholders until such deficiency shall be made good; and in case of such deficiency, the Comptroller of the Currency may compel said banking association to close its business and wind up its affairs under the provisions of this act.

And the Comptroller shall have authority to withhold from an association his certificate authorizing the commencement of business, whenever he shall have reason to suppose that the shareholders thereof have formed the same for any other than the legitimate objects contemplated by this act.

Comptroller may withhold certificate in certain cases.

Sec. 13. *And be it further enacted*, That it shall be lawful for any association formed under this act, by its articles of association, to provide for an increase of its capital from time to time as may be deemed expedient, subject to the limitations of this act: *Provided*, That the maximum of such increase in the articles of association shall be determined by the Comptroller of the Currency; and no increase of capital shall be valid until the whole amount of such increase shall be paid in, and notice thereof shall have been transmitted to the Comptroller of the Currency, and his certificate obtained specifying the amount of such increase of capital stock, with his approval thereof, and that it has been duly paid in as part of the capital of such association.

Increase of capital.

And every association shall have power, by the vote of shareholders owning two-thirds of its capital stock, to reduce the capital of such association to any sum not below the amount required by this act, in the formation of associations: *Provided*, That by no such reduction shall its capital be brought below the amount required by this act for its outstanding circulation, nor shall any such reduction be made until the amount of the proposed reduction has been reported to the Comptroller of the Currency and his approval thereof obtained.

Reduction of capital.

Proviso.

Sec. 14. *And be it further enacted*, That at least fifty per centum of the capital stock of every association shall be paid

Fifty per cent. of capital to be paid in—

Before commencing business.

in before it shall be authorized to commence business; and the remainder of the capital stock of such association shall be paid in installments of at least ten per centum each on the whole amount of the capital as frequently as one installment at the end of each succeeding month from the time it shall be authorized by the Comptroller to commence business; and the payment of each installment shall be certified to the Comptroller, under oath, by the president or cashier of the association.

Stock of delinquent stockholders, how sold.

SEC. 15. *And be it further enacted*, That if any shareholder, or his assignee, shall fail to pay any installment on the stock when the same is required by the foregoing section to be paid, the directors of such association may sell the stock of such delinquent shareholder at public auction, having given three weeks' previous notice thereof in a newspaper published and of general circulation in the city or county where the association is located, and if no newspaper is published in said city or county, then in a newspaper published nearest thereto, to any person who will pay the highest price therefor, and not less than the amount then due thereon, with the expenses of advertisement and sale; and the excess, if any, shall be paid to the delinquent shareholder.

If no bidder can be found who will pay for such stock the amount due thereon to the association, and the cost of advertisement and sale, the amount previously paid shall be forfeited to the association, and such stock shall be sold, as the directors may order, within six months from the time of such forfeiture, and if not sold it shall be canceled and deducted from the capital stock of the association; and if such cancellation and reduction shall reduce the capital of the association below the minimum of capital required by this act, the capital stock shall, within thirty days from the date of such cancellation, be increased to the requirements of the act; in default of which a receiver may be appointed to close up the business of the association according to the provisions of the fiftieth section of this act.

DEPOSIT OF UNITED STATES BONDS.

Bonds to be deposited—

SEC. 16. *And be it further enacted*, That every association, after having complied with the provisions of this act, preliminary to the commencement of banking business under its provisions, and before it shall be authorized to commence business, shall transfer and deliver to the Treasurer of the United States any United States registered bonds bearing interest to an amount not less than thirty thousand dollars nor less than one-third of the capital stock paid in, which bonds shall be deposited with the Treasurer of the United States, and by him safely kept in his office until the same shall be otherwise disposed of in pursuance of the provisions of this act;

—before commencing business.

And the Secretary of the Treasury is hereby authorized to receive and cancel any United States coupon bonds, and to issue in lieu thereof registered bonds of like amount, bearing a like rate of interest, and having the same time to run; and the deposit of bonds shall be, by every association, increased as its capital may be paid up or increased, so that every association shall at all times have on deposit with the Treasurer registered United States bonds to the amount of at least one-third of its capital stock actually paid in:

*Provided*, That nothing in this section shall prevent an association that may desire to reduce its capital or to close up its business and dissolve its organization from taking up its bonds upon returning to the Comptroller its circulating notes in the proportion hereinafter named in this act, nor from taking up any excess of bonds beyond one-third of its capital stock and upon which no circulating notes have been delivered.

### CERTIFICATE OF ORGANIZATION.

Examination by Comptroller preliminary to issuing certificate.

SEC. 17. *And be it further enacted*, That whenever a certificate shall have been transmitted to the Comptroller of the Currency, as provided in this act, and the association transmitting the same shall notify the Comptroller that at least fifty per centum of its capital stock has been paid in as aforesaid, and that such association has complied with all the provisions of this act as required to be complied with before such association shall be authorized to commence the business of banking, the Comptroller shall examine into the condition of such association, ascertain especially the amount of money paid in on account of its capital, the name and place of residence of each of the directors of such association, and the amount of the capital stock of which each is the bona fide owner, and generally whether such association has complied with all the requirements of this act to entitle it to engage in the business of banking; and shall cause to be made and attested, by the oaths of a majority of the directors and by the president or cashier of such association, a statement of all the facts necessary to enable the Comptroller to determine whether such association is lawfully entitled to commence the business of banking under this act.

When certificate is to be issued by Comptroller.

SEC. 18. *And be it further enacted,* That if, upon a careful examination of the facts so reported, and of any other facts which may come to the knowledge of the Comptroller, whether by means of a special commission appointed by him for the purpose of inquiring into the condition of such association or otherwise, it shall appear that such association is lawfully entitled to commence the business of banking, the Comptroller shall give to such association a certificate, under his hand and official seal, that such association has complied with all the provisions of this act required to be complied with before being entitled to commence the business of banking under it, and that such association is authorized to commence said business accordingly; and it shall be the duty of the association to cause said certificate to be published in some newspaper published in the city or county where the association is located for at least sixty days next after the issuing thereof: *Provided,* That if no newspaper is published in such city or county, the certificate shall be published in a newspaper published nearest thereto.

—publication thereof.

TRANSFER OF BONDS TO TREASURER.

Transfer of bonds deposited—how made.

SEC. 19. *And be it further enacted,* That all transfers of United States bonds which shall be made by any association under the provisions of this act shall be made to the Treasurer of the United States in trust for the association, with a memorandum written or printed on each bond, and signed by the cashier or some other officer of the association making the deposit, a receipt therefor to be given to said association, or by the Comptroller of the Currency, or by a clerk appointed by him for that purpose, stating that it is held in trust for the association on whose behalf such transfer is made, and as security for the redemption and payment of any circulating notes that have been or may be delivered to such association.

Comptroller to countersign transfers:

No assignment or transfer of any such bonds by the Treasurer shall be deemed valid or of binding force and effect unless countersigned by the Comptroller of the Currency. It shall be the duty of the Comptroller of the Currency to keep in his office a book in which shall be entered the name of every association from whose accounts such transfer of bonds is made by the Treasurer, and the name of the party to whom such transfer is made; and the par value of the bonds so transferred shall be entered therein; and it shall be the duty of the Comptroller, immediately upon countersigning and entering the same, to advise by mail the association from whose account such transfer was made of the kind and numerical designation of the bonds and the amount thereof so transferred.

—keep transfer books:

—and notify parties:

—to have access to Treasurer's books, and Treasurer to his books.

SEC. 20. *And be it further enacted*, That it shall be the duty of the Comptroller of the Currency to countersign and enter in the book, in the manner aforesaid, every transfer or assignment of any bonds held by the Treasurer presented for his signature; and the Comptroller shall have at all times during office hours access to the books of the treasurer, for the purpose of ascertaining the correctness of the transfer or assignment presented to him to countersign; and the Treasurer shall have the like access to the book above mentioned, kept by the Comptroller, during office hours, to ascertain the correctness of the entries in the same; and the Comptroller shall also at all times have access to the bonds on deposit with the Treasurer, to ascertain their amount and condition.

## CIRCULATING NOTES.

Circulating notes to be delivered to banks, amount, proportion, &c.

SEC. 21. *And be it further enacted*, That upon the transfer and delivery of bonds to the Treasurer, as provided in the foregoing section, the association making the same shall be entitled to receive from the Comptroller of the Currency circulating notes of different denominations in blank, registered and countersigned as hereinafter provided, equal in amount to ninety per centum of the current market value of the United States bonds so transferred and delivered, but not exceeding ninety per centum of the amount of said bonds at the par value thereof, if bearing interest at a rate not less than five per centum per annum; and the amount of such circulating notes to be furnished to each association shall be in proportion to its paid-up capital, as follows, and no more:

To each association whose capital shall not exceed five hundred thousand dollars, ninety per centum of such capital;

To each association whose capital exceeds five hundred thousand dollars, but does not exceed one million dollars, eighty per centum of such capital;

To each association whose capital exceeds one million dollars, but does not exceed three millions of dollars, seventy-five per centum of such capital;

To each association whose capital exceeds three millions of dollars, sixty per centum of such capital;

Apportionment of circulation among the States.

And that one hundred and fifty millions of dollars of the entire amount of circulating notes authorized to be issued shall be apportioned to associations in the States, in the District of Columbia, and in the Territories, according to representative population, and the remainder shall be apportioned by the Secretary of the Treasury among associations formed in the several States, in the District of Columbia, and in the Territories,[8] having due regard to the existing banking capital, resource, and business of such State, District, and Territory. [*As amended by act of March* 3, 1865, *chapter* 82.]

Limitation of amount.

SEC. 22. *And be it further enacted*, That the entire amount of notes for circulation to be issued under this act shall not exceed three hundred millions of dollars.[9]

8. The act of July 12, 1870, chapter 252, section 6, provides for a re-distribution of $25,000,000 of circulation, to be taken from the banks of States having an excess, and given to those of States having less than their proportion.

9. The amount of currency notes which may be issued is increased $54,-000,000 by the act of July 12, 1870, section 1, to be apportioned as therein

In order to furnish suitable notes for circulation, the Comptroller of the Currency is hereby authorized and required, under the direction of the Secretary of the Treasury, to cause plates and dies to be engraved, in the best manner to guard against counterfeiting and fraudulent alterations, and to have printed therefrom and numbered such quantity of circulating notes, in blank, of the denominations of one dollar, two dollars, three dollars, five dollars, ten dollars, twenty dollars, fifty dollars, one hundred dollars, five hundred dollars, and one thousand dollars, as may be required to supply, under this act, the associations entitled to receive the same;

**Plates and dies, printing, &c.**

**Denomination of notes.**

Which notes shall express upon their face that they are secured by United States bonds, deposited with the Treasurer of the United States by the written or engraved signatures of the Treasurer and Register, and by the imprint of the seal of the Treasury; and shall also express upon their face the promise of the association receiving the same to pay on demand, attested by the signatures of the president or vice president and cashier. And the said notes shall bear such devices and such other statements, and shall be in such form, as the Secretary of the Treasury shall by regulation direct:

**Notes, what to express.**

*Provided,* That not more than one-sixth part of the notes furnished to an association shall be of a less denomination than five dollars, and that after specie payments shall be resumed no association shall be furnished with notes of a less denomination than five dollars.

**Limit to number of notes under $5.**

SEC. 23. *And be it further enacted,* That after any such association shall have caused its promise to pay such notes on demand to be signed by the president or vice president and cashier thereof, in such manner as to make them obligatory promissory notes, payable on demand, at its place of business, such association is hereby authorized to issue and circulate the same as money;

**When banks may issue the notes.**

---

provided; and no banking association organized after that date can have a circulation of currency notes in excess of $500,000.

A national gold bank may have a circulation of gold notes to an amount not exceeding $1,000,000, and there is no limit to the aggregate amount which may be issued. (*See Act of July* 12, 1870, *chapter* 252, *sec.* 3.)

For what the notes are receivable.

And the same shall be received at par in all parts of the United States in payment of taxes, excises, public lands, and all other dues to the United States, except for duties on imports; and also for all salaries and other debts and demands owing by the United States to individuals, corporations, and associations within the United States, except interest on the public debt, and in redemption of the national currency.

Banks to issue no other notes.

And no such association shall issue post notes or any other notes to circulate as money than such as are authorized by the foregoing provisions of this act.

Replacing of worn-out, mutilated, or lost notes.

SEC. 24. *And be it further enacted*, That it shall be the duty of the Comptroller of the Currency to receive worn-out or mutilated circulating notes issued by any such banking association, and also, on due proof of the destruction of any such circulating notes, to deliver in place thereof to such association other blank circulating notes to an equal amount.

Mutilated notes, &c., to be burned.

And such worn-out or mutilated notes, after a memorandum shall have been entered in the proper books, in accordance with such regulations as may be established by the Comptroller, as well as all circulating notes which shall have been paid or surrendered to be canceled, shall be burned to ashes in presence of four persons, one to be appointed by the Secretary of the Treasury, one by the Comptroller of the Currency, one by the Treasurer of the United States, and one by the association, under such regulations as the Secretary of the Treasury may prescribe. And a certificate of such burning, signed by the parties so appointed, shall be made in the books of the Comptroller, and a duplicate thereof forwarded to the association whose notes are thus canceled.

PROVISION CONCERNING BONDS HELD BY TREASURER.

Bonds to be examined annually by agents of banks.

SEC. 25. *And be it further enacted*, That it shall be the duty of every banking association having bonds deposited in the office of the Treasurer of the United States, once or oftener in each fiscal year, and at such time or times during the ordinary business hours as said officer or officers may select, to examine and compare the bonds so pledged with the books of the Comptroller and the accounts of the association, and, if found correct, to execute to the said Treasurer a certificate setting forth the different kinds and the amounts thereof, and that the same are in the possession and custody of the Treasurer at the date of such certificate. Such examination may be made by an officer or agent of such association, duly appointed in writing for that purpose, whose certificate before mentioned shall be of like force and validity as if executed by such president or cashier; and a duplicate signed by the Treasurer shall be retained by the association.

Bonds to be held exclusively for redemption of notes.

SEC. 26. *And be it further enacted,* That the bonds transferred to and deposited with the Treasurer of the United States, as hereinbefore provided, by any banking association for the security of its circulating notes, shall be held exclusively for that purpose, until such notes shall be redeemed, except as provided in this act;

—interest on, payable to the banks.

But the Comptroller of the Currency shall give to any such banking association powers of attorney to receive and appropriate to its own use the interest on the bonds which it shall have so transferred to the Treasurer; but such powers shall become inoperative whenever such banking association shall fail to redeem its circulating notes as aforesaid.

—when market value falls below amount of circulation, additional bonds to be deposited.

Whenever the market or cash value of any bonds deposited with the Treasurer of the United States, as aforesaid, shall be reduced below the amount of the circulation issued for the same, the Comptroller of the Currency is hereby authorized to demand and receive the amount of such depreciation in other United States bonds at cash value, or in money, from the association receiving said bills, to be deposited with the Treasurer of the United States as long as such depreciation continues.

—may be exchanged for other bonds.

And said Comptroller, upon the terms prescribed by the Secretary of the Treasury, may permit an exchange to be made of any of the bonds deposited with the Treasurer by an association for other bonds of the United States authorized by this act to be received as security for circulating notes, if he shall be of opinion that such an exchange can be made without prejudice to the United States, and he may direct the return of any of said bonds to the banking association which transferred the same, in sums of not less than one thousand dollars, upon the surrender to him and the cancellation of a proportionate amount of such circulating notes:

*Provided*, That the remaining bonds which shall have been transferred by the banking association offering to surrender circulating notes shall be equal to the amount required for the circulating notes not surrendered by such banking association, and that the amount of bonds in the hands of the Treasurer shall not be diminished below the amount required to be kept on deposit with him by this act:

*And provided*, That there shall have been no failure by such association to redeem its circulating notes, and no other violation by such association of the provisions of this act, and that the market or cash value of the remaining bonds shall not be below the amount required for the circulation issued for the same.

Unlawful issue of notes to associations—penalty incurred.

SEC. 27. *And be it further enacted*, That it shall be unlawful for any officer acting under the provisions of this act to countersign or deliver to any association, or to any other company or person, any circulating notes contemplated by this act, except as hereinbefore provided, and in accordance with the true intent and meaning of this act. And any officer who shall violate the provisions of this section shall be deemed guilty of a high misdemeanor, and on conviction thereof shall be punished by fine not exceeding double the amount so countersigned and delivered, and imprisonment not less than one year and not exceeding fifteen years, at the discretion of the court in which he shall be tried.

### BANKS MAY HOLD REAL ESTATE.

Banks may hold and convey real estate.

SEC. 28. *And be it further enacted*, That it shall be lawful for any such association to purchase, hold, and convey real estate as follows:—

—to what extent.

First. Such as shall be necessary for its immediate accommodation in the transaction of its business.

Second. Such as shall be mortgaged to it in good faith by way of security for debts previously contracted.

Third. Such as shall be conveyed to it in satisfaction of debts previously contracted in the course of its dealings.

Fourth. Such as it shall purchase at sales under judgments, decrees, or mortgages held by such association, or shall purchase to secure debts due to said association.

And such association shall not purchase or hold real estate in any other case or for any other purpose than as specified in this section. Nor shall it hold the possession of any real estate under mortgage, or hold the title and possession of any real estate purchased to secure any debts due to it for a longer period than five years. General limitation.

### LOANS AND DISCOUNTS.

SEC. 29. *And be it further enacted,* That the total liabilities to any association, of any person, or of any company, corporation, or firm for money borrowed, including in the liabilities of a company or firm the liabilities of the several members thereof, shall at no time exceed one-tenth part of the amount of the capital stock of such association actually paid in: *Provided,* That the discount of bona fide bills of exchange drawn against actually existing values, and the discount of commercial or business paper actually owned by the person or persons, corporation, or firm negotiating the same, shall not be considered as money borrowed. Loans limited.

SEC. 30. *And be it further enacted,* That every association may take, receive, reserve, and charge, on any loan or discount made, or upon any note, bill of exchange, or other evidences of debt, interest at the rate allowed by the laws of the State or Territory where the bank is located, and no more, except that where by the laws of any State a different rate is limited for banks of issue organized under State laws, the rates so limited shall be allowed for associations organized in any such State under this act. Interest on loans and discounts.

And when no rate is fixed by the laws of the State or Territory, the bank may take, receive, reserve, or charge a rate not exceeding seven per centum, and such interest may be taken in advance, reckoning the days for which the note, bill, or other evidence of debt has to run.

And the knowingly taking, receiving, reserving, or charg- Excessive rates—

—penalties incurred.

ing a rate of interest greater than aforesaid shall be held and adjudged a forfeiture of the entire interest which the note, bill, or other evidence of debt carries with it, or which has been agreed to be paid thereon. And in case a greater rate of interest has been paid, the person or persons paying the same, or their legal representatives, may recover back, in any action of debt, twice the amount of the interest thus paid from the association taking or receiving the same: *Provided*, That such action is commenced within two years from the time the usurious transaction occurred.

Exchange may be charged.

But the purchase, discount, or sale of a bona fide bill of exchange, payable at another place than the place of such purchase, discount, or sale, at not more than the current rate of exchange for sight drafts in addition to the interest, shall not be considered as taking or receiving a greater rate of interest.

LEGAL RESERVES REQUIRED.

Banks to hold certain reserves.

SEC. 31. *And be it further enacted*, That every association in the cities hereinafter named shall at all times have on hand, in lawful money of the United States, an amount equal to at least twenty-five per centum of the aggregate amount of its notes in circulation and its deposits; and every other association shall, at all times, have on hand, in lawful money of the United States, an amount equal to at least fifteen per centum of the aggregate amount of its notes in circulation and of its deposits.[10]

In case of deficiency—

And whenever the lawful money of any association in any of the cities hereinafter named shall be below the amount of twenty-five per centum of its circulation and deposits, and whenever the lawful money of any other association shall be below fifteen per centum of its circulation and de-

10. By the act of March 2, 1867, chapter 194, the temporary loan certificates, or three per cent. certificates, authorized by that act, may be held as part of the national bank reserves, subject to the limitation that not less than two-fifths of the entire reserve of any bank shall consist of lawful money of the United States.

And by act of June 8, 1872, chapter 346, the certificates of deposit therein provided for, to be issued in exchange for United States notes, may be held as part of the legal reserves of banks, and may be accepted in the settlement of clearing-house balances. (*See pp.* 27, 28.)

posits, such association shall not increase its liabilities by making any new loans or discounts otherwise than by discounting or purchasing bills of exchange payable at sight, nor make any dividend of its profits until the required proportion between the aggregate amount of its outstanding notes of circulation and deposits and its lawful money of the United States shall be restored:

—certain restrictions imposed.

*Provided*, That three-fifths of said fifteen per centum may consist of balances due to an association available for the redemption of its circulating notes from associations approved by the Comptroller of the Currency, organized under this act, in the cities of Saint Louis, Louisville, Chicago, Detroit, Milwaukee, New Orleans, Cincinnati, Cleveland, Pittsburg, Baltimore, Philadelphia, Boston, New York, Albany, *Leavenworth*,* San Francisco, and Washington city:

*Provided, also*, That clearing-house certificates, representing specie or lawful money specially deposited for the purpose of any clearing-house association, shall be deemed to be lawful money in the possession of any association belonging to such clearing-house holding and owning such certificate, and shall be considered to be a part of the lawful money which such association is required to have under the foregoing provisions of this section:

*Provided*, That the cities of Charleston and Richmond may be added to the list of cities in the national associations of which other associations may keep three-fifths of their lawful money, whenever, in the opinion of the Comptroller of the Currency, the condition of the southern States will warrant it.

In default of sufficient reserve, after notice, bank may be wound up.

And it shall be competent for the Comptroller of the Currency to notify any association whose lawful money reserve as aforesaid shall be below the amount to be kept on hand as aforesaid, to make good such reserve; and if such association shall fail for thirty days thereafter so to make good its reserve of lawful money of the United States, the Comptroller may, with the concurrence of the Secretary of the Treasury, appoint a receiver[11] to wind up the business of such association, as provided in this act.

* Leavenworth is stricken out by act of March 1, 1872.

11. See section 50, and notes thereto, pp. 133, 134.

REDEMPTION AGENCIES.

Redemption agencies at New York to be selected—

Sec. 32. *And be it further enacted*, That each association organized in any of the cities named in the foregoing section shall select, subject to the approval of the Comptroller of the Currency, an association in the city of New York at which it will redeem its circulating notes at par.[12] And each of such associations may keep one-half of its lawful money reserve in cash deposits in the city of New York.

—where part of reserves may be kept.

Like agencies in other cities.

And each association not organized within the cities named in the preceding section shall select, subject to the approval of the Comptroller of the Currency, an association in either of the cities named in the preceding section at which it will redeem its circulating notes at par, and the Comptroller shall give public notice of the names of the associations so selected at which redemptions are to be made by the respective associations, and of any change that may be made of the association at which the notes of any association are redeemed.

Banks to redeem their own notes at par,

and to receive the notes of any other national bank in payment of debts, &c.

If any association shall fail either to make the selection or to redeem its notes as aforesaid, the Comptroller of the Currency may, upon receiving satisfactory evidence thereof, appoint a receiver, in the manner provided for in this act, to wind up its affairs: *Provided*, That nothing in this section shall relieve any association from its liability to redeem its circulating notes at its own counter, at par, in lawful money, on demand: *And provided further*, That every association formed or existing under the provisions of this act shall take and receive at par,[12] for any debt or liability to said association, any and all notes or bills issued by any association existing under and by virtue of this act.

DIVIDENDS.

Dividends, when and how declared.

Sec. 33. *And be it further enacted*, That the directors of any association may, semi-annually, each year, declare a

12. The act of July 12, 1870, chapter 252, section 5, exempts gold banks in San Francisco from any obligation to redeem their gold notes at par in the city of New York, and also exempts all gold banks from the provision requiring national banks to receive in payment of debts the currency notes of every other bank at par.

dividend of so much of the net profits of the association as they shall judge expedient; but each association shall, before the declaration of a dividend, carry one-tenth part of its net profits of the preceding half year to its surplus fund, until the same shall amount to twenty per centum of its capital stock.[13] Restriction.

SEC. 34. [*Relating to reports, superseded by act of March* 3, 1869, *chapter* 130.]

### PURCHASING AND LOANING ON SHARES.

SEC. 35. *And be it further enacted*, That no association shall make any loan or discount on the security of the shares of its own capital stock,[14] nor be the purchaser or holder of any such shares, unless such security or purchase shall be necessary to prevent loss upon a debt previously contracted in good faith; and stock so purchased or acquired shall, within six months from the time of its purchase, be sold or disposed of at public or private sale, in default of which a receiver may be appointed to close up the business of the association, according to the provisions of this act. Banks not to loan on, purchase, or hold their own shares, except in certain cases.

### LIMITATIONS AND RESTRICTIONS.

SEC. 36. *And be it further enacted*, That no association shall at any time be indebted, or in any way liable, to an amount exceeding the amount of its capital stock at such time actually paid in and remaining undiminished by losses or otherwise, except on the following accounts, that is to say— Limitation of indebtedness and exceptions.

First. On account of its notes of circulation.

Second. On account of moneys deposited with, or collected by, such association.

Third. On account of bills of exchange or drafts drawn against money actually on deposit to the credit of such association or due thereto.

---

13. There are further restrictions in section 38, on making dividends, that none shall be made to a greater amount than the net profits on hand, and none whatever if the losses equal or exceed the profits.

14. The deposit of funds of a bank with bankers is a loan within the meaning of this section, and cannot be secured by a pledge of the shares of the bank. (*Bank* v. *Lanier*, 11 *Wallace*, 369.)

Fourth. On account of liabilities to its stockholders for dividends and reserved profits.

Notes not to be pledged nor used to increase capital.

SEC. 37. *And be it further enacted*, That no association shall, either directly or indirectly, pledge or hypothecate any of its notes of circulation, for the purpose of procuring money to be paid in on its capital stock, or to be used in its banking operations, or otherwise; nor shall any association use its circulating notes, or any part thereof, in any manner or form, to create or increase its capital stock.

Withdrawal of capital forbidden.

SEC. 38. *And be it further enacted*, That no association, or any member thereof, shall, during the time it shall continue its banking operations, withdraw, or permit to be withdrawn, either in form of dividends or otherwise, any portion of its capital.

Dividends limited when losses occur by bad debts.

And if losses shall at any time have been sustained by any such association equal to or exceeding its undivided profits then on hand, no dividend shall be made; and no dividend shall ever be made by any association, while it shall continue its banking operations, to an amount greater than its net profits then on hand, deducting therefrom its losses and bad debts.

What are bad debts.

And all debts due to any association, on which interest is past due and unpaid for a period of six months, unless the same shall be well secured, and shall be in process of collection, shall be considered bad debts within the meaning of this act: *Provided*, That nothing in this section shall prevent the reduction of the capital stock of the association under the thirteenth section of this act.

Notes not to be paid out, except those of solvent banks, redeemable at par.

SEC. 39. *And be it further enacted*, That no association shall at any time pay out on loans or discounts, or in purchasing drafts or bills of exchange, or in payment of deposits, or in any other mode pay or put in circulation the notes of any bank or banking association which shall not, at any such time, be receivable, at par, on deposit and in payment of debts by the association so paying out or circulating such notes; nor shall it knowingly pay out or put in circulation any notes issued by any bank or banking association which at the time of such paying out or putting in circulation is not redeeming its circulating notes in lawful money of the United States.

LIST OF STOCKHOLDERS.

SEC. 40. *And be it further enacted*, That the president and cashier of every such association shall cause to be kept at all times a full and correct list of the names and residences of all the shareholders in the association, and the number of shares held by each, in the office where its business is transacted; and such list shall be subject to the inspection of all the shareholders and creditors of the association, and the officers authorized to assess taxes under State authority, during business hours of each day in which business may be legally transacted; and a copy of such list, on the first Monday of July in each year, verified by the oath of such president or cashier, shall be transmitted to the Comptroller of the Currency.

List of stockholders to be kept at all times and sent to Comptroller annually.

PLATES AND DIES—TAXES.

SEC. 41. *And be it further enacted*, That the plates and special dies to be procured by the Comptroller of the Currency for the printing of such circulating notes shall remain under his control and direction, and the expenses necessarily incurred in executing the provisions of this act respecting the procuring of such notes, and all other expenses of the bureau, shall be paid out of the proceeds of the taxes or duties now or hereafter to be assessed on the circulation, and collected from associations organized under this act.

Plates and dies, how kept.

And in lieu of all existing taxes, every association shall pay to the Treasurer of the United States, in the months of January and July, a duty [15] of one-half of one per centum each half year from and after the first day of January, eighteen hundred and sixty-four, upon the average amount of its notes in circulation, and a duty of one-quarter of one per centum each half year upon the average amount of its deposits, and a duty of one-quarter of one per centum each half year, as aforesaid, on the average amount of its capital

Duties or taxes to be paid by banks.

15. The regulations and instructions of the Treasury Department in relation to the payment of taxes and duties by banks may be found at the end of the banking laws printed in this volume.

stock beyond the amount invested in United States bonds; and in case of default in the payment thereof by any association, the duties aforesaid may be collected in the manner provided for the collection of United States duties of other corporations, or the Treasurer may reserve the amount of said duties out of the interest, as it may become due on the bonds deposited with him by such defaulting association.

Semi-annual returns.

And it shall be the duty of each association, within ten days from the first days of January and July of each year, to make a return, under the oath of its president or cashier, to the Treasurer of the United States, in such form as he may prescribe, of the average amount of its notes in circulation, and of the average amount of its deposits, and of the average amount of its capital stock, beyond the amount invested in United States bonds, for the six months next preceding said first days of January and July as aforesaid, and in default of such return, and for each default thereof, each defaulting association shall forfeit and pay to the United States the sum of two hundred dollars, to be collected either out of the interest as it may become due such association on the bonds deposited with the Treasurer, or, at his option, in the manner in which penalties are to be collected of other corporations under the laws of the United States; and in case of such default the amount of the duties to be paid by such association shall be assessed upon the amount of notes delivered to such association by the Comptroller of the Currency, and upon the highest amount of its deposits and capital stock, to be ascertained in such other manner as the Treasurer may deem best:

Penalty for default.

Taxes on shares may be imposed by State authority.

*Provided*, That nothing in this act shall be construed to prevent all the shares in any of the said associations, held by any person or body corporate, from being included in the valuation of the personal property of such person or corporation in the assessment of taxes imposed by or under State authority[16] at the place where such bank is located, and

16. By act of Feb'y 10, 1868, chapter 7, the word "place," as used in this section, is defined to mean the State within which the bank is located, and further provisions are made authorizing States to tax national banks.

Bank shares may constitutionally be taxed under State authority, with

not elsewhere, but not at a greater rate than is assessed upon other moneyed capital in the hands of individual citizens of such State: *Provided further*, That the tax so imposed under the laws of any State upon the shares of any of the associations authorized by this act shall not exceed the rate imposed upon the shares in any of the banks organized under authority of the State where such association is located: *Provided, also*, That nothing in this act shall exempt the real estate of associations from either State, county, or municipal taxes to the same extent, according to its value, as other real estate is taxed.

And on real estate.

### LIQUIDATION AND CLOSING

SEC. 12. *And be it further enacted*, That any association may go into liquidation and be closed by the vote of its shareholders owning two-thirds of its stock. And whenever such vote shall be taken, it shall be the duty of the

Banks may voluntarily go into liquidation.

---

out regard to the fact that part or the whole of the capital of the bank is invested in obligations of the United States exempt by law from taxation; but an act of the State of New York authorizing taxation of national bank shares, which did not contain a limitation that the tax so authorized should not exceed the rate imposed upon the shares of any of the banks organized under authority of the State, which latter banks were taxed on their capital but not on their shares, was held to be void. (*Van Allen* v. *The Assessors*, 3 *Wallace*, 573; *People* v. *The Commissioners*, 4 *Wallace*, 244; *Bradley* v. *The People*, 4 *Wallace*, 459.)

A State law, requiring national banks to pay the taxes rightfully assessed upon the shares of its stock, is valid. (*National Bank* v. *Commonwealth*, 9 *Wallace*, 353.)

The State of Missouri had two banks of issue, which it had by contract exempted from taxation beyond a limited amount. It had many other banks not of issue, which were by law taxed at a greater amount. *Held*, that the shares of national banks in that State might be taxed at as high a rate as those of the State banks whose taxation was not limited. (*Lionberger* v. *Rouse*, 9 *Wallace*, 468.)

There is much conflict of opinion in the numerous decisions of State courts in relation to the taxation of national banks, which it would be of little practical advantage to undertake to specify here, as those opinions are binding only in the States where given, and not there even when contrary to the decisions of the Supreme Court of the United States.

They may be found in 53 *Maine*, 594; 55 *Maine*, 456; 56 *Maine*, 274, 310; 99 *Mass.*, 141; 14 *Allen*, 359; 11 *Minn.*, 500; 44 *Barbour*, 148; 32 *Conn.*, 173; 16 *Ohio State R.*, 614; 54 *Penn. State R.*, 139; 23 *Wis.*, 655; 27 *Iowa*, 350; 32 *New Jersey Law R.*, 273. (*See also* 2 *Black*, *S. C. U. S.*, 620.)

board of directors to cause notice of this fact to be certified, under the seal of the association, by its president or cashier, to the Comptroller of the Currency, and publication thereof to be made for a period of two months in a newspaper published in the city of New York, and also in a newspaper published in a city or town in which the association is located, and if no newspaper be there published, then in the newspaper published nearest thereto, that said association is closing up its affairs, and notifying the holders of its notes and other creditors to present the notes and other claims against the association for payment.

And after one year, on payment of outstanding notes, may withdraw its bonds.

And at any time after the expiration of one year from the time of the publication of such notice as aforesaid, the said association may pay over to the Treasurer of the United States the amount of its outstanding notes in the lawful money of the United States, and take up the bonds which said association has on deposit with the Treasurer for the security of its circulating notes;[17] which bonds shall be assigned to the bank in the manner specified in the nineteenth section of this act, and from that time the outstanding notes of said association shall be redeemed at the Treasury of the United States, and the said association and the shareholders thereof shall be discharged from all liabilities therefor.

Redemption account to be kept by Treasurer; notes to be redeemed and burned

SEC. 43. *And be it further enacted,* That the Treasurer, on receiving from an association lawful money for the payment and redemption of its outstanding notes, as provided for in the preceding section of this act, shall execute duplicate receipts therefor, one to the association and the other to the Comptroller of the Currency, stating the amount received by him, and the purpose for which it has been received, which amount shall be paid into the Treasury of the United States, and placed to the credit of such association upon redemption account. And it shall be the duty of the Treasurer, whenever he shall redeem any of the notes of said association, to cause the same to be mutilated, and charged to the redemption account of said association; and

---

17. Banks are *required* to do this within *six months* after voting to go into liquidation. (*See page* 157, *act of July* 14, 1870.) Bonds deposited to secure circulation cannot be retained for other claims of the United States. (*Opinions of Attorneys General, vol.* 12, *p.* 549.)

all notes so redeemed by the Treasurer shall, every three months, be certified to and burned in the manner prescribed in the twenty-fourth section of this act.

## CONVERSION OF STATE BANKS.

State banks, how they may become national banks.

SEC. 44. *And be it further enacted*, That any bank incorporated by special law, or any banking institution organized under a general law of any State,[18] may, by authority of this act, become a national association under its provisions, by the name prescribed in its organization certificate; and in such case the articles of association and the organization certificate required by this act may be executed by a majority of the directors of the bank or banking institution; and said certificate shall declare that the owners of two-thirds of the capital stock have authorized the directors to make such certificate and to change and convert the said bank or banking institution into a national association under this act.

And a majority of the directors, after executing said articles of association and organization certificate, shall have power to execute all other papers, and to do whatever may be required to make its organization perfect and complete as a national association.

Shares of stock may remain the same.

The shares of any such bank may continue to be for the same amount each as they were before said conversion, and

---

18. A national bank organized from a State bank, and receiving its assets, is liable for its debts. (*Thorp* v. *Wegefarth*, 56 *Penn.*, 82.)

The right of action to recover damages for the fraudulent misapplication of the property of a State bank by one of its officers passes as assets to the national bank into which it is converted under this act. (*Grocers' National Bank of the City of New York* v. *Clarke*, 48 *Barbour*, 26.)

For minimum amount of capital allowed see section 7, page 104.

The act of March 3, 1865, (*chapter* 78, *section* 7,) authorizes State banks having branches to be converted into national banks, and to keep their branches in operation.

That part of section 7 above referred to which allowed State banks for a limited time to become national associations, in preference to new organizations, is omitted, because the time limited has expired.

National banks cannot become State banks and cease to be national, without authority of Congress therefor, which does not now exist. (*Official Opinion of Attorney General Hoar*, 1869.)

Directors.

the directors aforesaid may be the directors of the association until others are elected or appointed in accordance with the provisions of this act;

May continue to hold shares in other banks.

And any State bank which is a stockholder in any other bank, by authority of State laws, may continue to hold its stock, although either bank, or both, may be organized under and have accepted the provisions of this act.

When may commence business.

When the Comptroller shall give to such association a certificate, under his hand and official seal, that the provisions of this act have been complied with, and that it is authorized to commence the business of banking under it, the association shall have the same powers and privileges, and shall be subject to the same duties, responsibilities, and rules, in all respects, as are prescribed in this act for other associations organized under it, and shall be held and regarded as an association under this act: *Provided, however,* That no such association shall have a less capital than the amount prescribed for banking associations under this act.

Minimum capital.

DESIGNATED DEPOSITARIES.

When may be depositaries of public moneys.

SEC. 45. *And be it further enacted,* That all associations under this act, when designated for that purpose by the Secretary of the Treasury, shall be depositaries of public money,[19] except receipts from customs, under such regulations as may be prescribed by the Secretary; and they may also be employed as financial agents of the Government; and they shall perform all such reasonable duties, as depositaries of public moneys and financial agents of the Government, as may be required of them.

Security to be given.

And the Secretary of the Treasury shall require of the associations thus designated satisfactory security, by the deposit of United States bonds and otherwise, for the safekeeping and prompt payment of the public money deposited

19. Banks designated as depositaries, under the provisions of this act, are public depositaries within the meaning of the act of August 6, 1846, (9 *Stat. at Large*, 59,) as amended by the act of March 3, 1857, (11 *Stat. at Large*, 249,) requiring every disbursing officer or agent of the United States, having any money of the Government, to deposit the same with the United States Treasurer, or with some one of the Assistant Treasurers or public depositaries. (*Opinions of Attorneys General, vol.* 11, *page* 29.)

with them, and for the faithful performance of their duties as financial agents of the Government: *Provided*, That every association which shall be selected and designated as receiver or depositary of the public money shall take and receive at par all of the national currency bills, by whatever association issued, which have been paid into the Government for internal revenue, or for loans or stocks.

To receive at par all national currency bills.

## PROCEEDINGS ON FAILURE TO REDEEM NOTES.

Notes, when not redeemed on demand by banks issuing them, to be protested.

SEC. 46. *And be it further enacted*, That if any association shall at any time fail to redeem, in the lawful money of the United States, any of its circulating notes, when payment thereof shall be lawfully demanded, during the usual hours of business, at the office of such association, or at its place of redemption aforesaid, the holder may cause the same to be protested, in one package, by a notary public, unless the president or cashier of the association whose notes are presented for payment, or the president or cashier of the association at the place at which they are redeemable, shall offer to waive demand and notice of the protest, and shall, in pursuance of such offer, make, sign, and deliver to the party making such demand an admission in writing, stating the time of the demand, the amount demanded, and the fact of the non-payment thereof; and such notary public, on making such protest, or upon receiving such admission, shall forthwith forward such admission or notice of protest to the Comptroller of the Currency, retaining a copy thereof.

Comptroller to examine into the facts and notify banks, &c.

And after such default, on examination of the facts by the Comptroller, and notice by him to the association, it shall not be lawful for the association suffering the same to pay out any of its notes, discount any notes or bills, or otherwise prosecute the business of banking, except to receive and safely keep money belonging to it, and to deliver special deposits:

Restriction on protest and fees therefor.

*Provided*, That if satisfactory proof be produced to such notary public that the payment of any such notes is restrained by order of any court of competent jurisdiction, such notary public shall not protest the same; and when the holder of such notes shall cause more than one note or package to be protested on the same day, he shall not receive pay for more than one protest.

Comptroller's duty on receiving notice of protest of notes.

SEC. 47. *And be it further enacted*, That on receiving notice that any such association has failed to redeem any of its circulating notes, as specified in the next preceding section, the Comptroller of the Currency, with the concurrence of the Secretary of the Treasury, may appoint a special agent (of whose appointment immediate notice shall be given to such association,) who shall immediately proceed to ascertain whether such association has refused to pay its circulating notes in the lawful money of the United States, when demanded as aforesaid, and report to the Comptroller the facts so ascertained; and if, from such protest or the report so made, the Comptroller shall be satisfied that such association has refused to pay its circulating notes as aforesaid and is in default, he shall, within thirty days after he shall have received notice of such failure, declare the United States bonds and securities pledged by such association forfeited to the United States, and the same shall thereupon be forfeited accordingly.

Forfeiture of bonds.

If bonds are forfeited, notes to be called in and paid at U. S. Treasury.

And thereupon the Comptroller shall immediately give notice in such manner as the Secretary of the Treasury shall, by general rules or otherwise, direct, to the holders of the circulating notes of such association to present them for payment at the Treasury of the United States, and the same shall be paid as presented in lawful money of the United States; whereupon said Comptroller may, in his discretion, cancel an amount of bonds pledged by such association equal at current market rates, not exceeding par, to the notes paid.

Disposal of notes redeemed.

And it shall be lawful for the Secretary of the Treasury, from time to time, to make such regulations respecting the disposition to be made of such circulating notes after presentation thereof for payment as aforesaid, and respecting the perpetuation of the evidence of the payment thereof, as may seem to him proper; but all such notes, on being paid, shall be canceled.

In case of deficiency—

And for any deficiency in the proceeds of the bonds pledged by such association, when disposed of as hereinafter specified, to reimburse to the United States the amount so expended in paying the circulating notes of such association, the United States shall have a first and paramount lien upon all the assets of such association; and such deficiency shall be made good out of such assets in preference to any and all other claims whatsoever, except the necessary costs and expenses of administering the same.

—United States to have prior lien on assets for amount expended in redemption of notes.

(See note 24, page 135.)

Bonds to be sold at auction for redemption of notes.

SEC. 48. *And be it further enacted*, That whenever the Comptroller shall become satisfied, as in the last preceding section specified, that any association has refused to pay its circulating notes as therein mentioned, he may, instead of canceling the United States bonds pledged by such association, as provided in the next preceding section, cause so much of them as may be necessary to redeem the outstanding circulating notes of such association to be sold at public auction in the city of New York, after giving thirty days' notice of such sale to such association.

May be sold at private sale if Comptroller thinks best.

SEC. 49. *And be it further enacted*, That the Comptroller of the Currency may, if he shall be of opinion that the interests of the United States will be best promoted thereby, sell at private sale any of the bonds pledged by such association, and receive therefor either money or the circulating notes of such failing association: *Provided*, That no such bonds shall be sold by private sale for less than par, nor less than the market value thereof at the time of sale:

Sales not complete until transfer made.

*And provided further*, That no sales of any such bonds, either public or private, shall be complete until the transfer thereof shall have been made with the formalities prescribed in this act.

Receiver, when to be appointed, his bond and duties.

SEC. 50. *And be it further enacted*, That on becoming satisfied, as specified in this act, that any association has refused to pay its circulating notes as therein mentioned, and is in default, the Comptroller of the Currency may forthwith appoint a receiver, and require of him such bond and security as he shall deem proper, who, under the direction of the Comptroller, shall take possession of the books, records, and assets [20] of every description of such associa-

---

20. As to the power of a receiver over the residue of bonds deposited to secure circulation, after the payment of all notes, see the opinions of

tion, collect all debts, dues, and claims [21] belonging to such association, and, upon the order of a court of record of competent jurisdiction,[22] may sell or compound all bad or doubtful debts, and, on a like order, sell all the real and personal property of such association, on such terms as the court shall direct; and may, if necessary to pay the debts of such association, enforce the individual liability of the stockholders provided for by the twelfth section of this act;[23] and such receiver shall pay over all money so made to the Treasurer of the United States, subject to the order of the

---

a divided court in *Van Antwerp* v. *Hulburd et al.*, (8 *Blatchford C. C. R.*, 282.)

The right to appeal from a judgment in a suit against a State bank converted into a national bank which fails, passes to the receiver. (*Claflin* v. *The Farmers and Citizens' Bank of Long Island*, 54 *Barbour*, 228.)

21. The word "debts" in this section includes all legal liabilities. The assets in the hands of the receiver are to be divided and appropriated to the payment of all legal liabilities, whether such liabilities are debts, technically so called, or result from the non-feasance or mal-feasance of the association in respect to its binding obligations and duties. (*Turner* v. *First National Bank of Keokuk*, 26 *Iowa*, 562.)

A receiver of a national bank is an officer of the United States, and may bring suits in the district courts of the United States, under the provisions of the act of March 3, 1815, (sec. 4,) to collect claims due to the bank. His appointment by the Comptroller of the Currency, with the concurrence of the Secretary of the Treasury, is equivalent to an appointment by the Secretary, who is the head of a Department, and comes within the provisions of the Constitution, art. II, sec. 2, sub. 2. (*Platt, Receiver*, v. *Beach*, 2 *Benedict's District Court R.*, 303.)

After a bank had stopped payment, and before a receiver was appointed, a debtor to the bank purchased and took an assignment of the claim of a depositor, for the purpose of having it set off against his debt. A receiver was afterwards appointed, and the set-off was disallowed and the assignment held to be void, as an attempt to give a preference probibited by this act. (*Venango National Bank* v. *Taylor*, 56 *Penn.*, 14.)

22. A district court of the United States is a court of record of competent jurisdiction, within the meaning of this section, to make an order authorizing a receiver to compromise doubtful debts. (*Petition of Platt, Receiver*, 1 *Benedict's District Court R.*, 534.)

23. Action on the part of the Comptroller of the Currency is indispensable, whenever the personal liability of the stockholders is sought to be enforced, and must precede the institution of suit by the receiver, who is the statutory assignee, and the proper party to institute all suits. Creditors of the bank are not proper parties to such suits. (*Kennedy* v. *Gibson et al.*, 8 *Wallace*, 498.)

Comptroller of the Currency, and also make report to the Comptroller of the Currency of all his acts and proceedings. The Comptroller shall thereupon cause notice to be given, by advertisement in such newspapers as he may direct, for three consecutive months, calling on all persons who may have claims against such association to present the same, and to make legal proof thereof. And from time to time the Comptroller, after full provision shall have been first made for refunding to the United States any such deficiency in redeeming the notes of such association as is mentioned in this act, shall make a ratable [24] dividend of the money so paid over to him by such receiver on all such claims as may have been proved to his satisfaction or adjudicated in a court of competent jurisdiction; [25] and from time to time, as the proceeds of the assets of such association shall be paid over to him, he shall make further dividends, as aforesaid, on all claims previously proved or adjudicated; and the remainder of such proceeds, if any, shall be paid over to the shareholders of such association, or their legal representatives, in proportion to the stock by them respectively held.

Comptroller to advertise for claims—

—and make dividends.

Balance, if any, to be paid to shareholders.

*Provided, however*, That if such association against which proceedings have been so instituted, on account of any alleged refusal to redeem its circulating notes as aforesaid, shall deny having failed to do so, such association may, at any time within ten days after such association shall have been notified of the appointment of an agent, as provided in this act, apply to the nearest circuit, or district, or territorial court of the United States, to enjoin further proceedings in the premises; and such court, after citing the

Banks denying that they have refused to redeem notes may appeal to U. S. courts.

24. The United States have no right to priority of payment of debts due to the Government as against private creditors of insolvent banks, except to be reimbursed the amount expended in redeeming the circulating notes of such banks, according to the provisions of section 47 of this act. (*See page* 132.)

The act of March 3, 1797, (sec. 5,) giving the United States priority over general creditors of insolvent debtors, does not apply to national banks. (*Official Opinion of Attorney General Akerman*, 1870.)

25. The Supreme Court of Iowa held that the receiver is a proper party in proceedings for the adjudication of claims against a national bank. (*Turner* v. *First National Bank of Keokuk*, 26 *Iowa*, 562.)

Comptroller of the Currency to show cause why further proceedings should not be enjoined, and after the decision of the court or finding of a jury that such association has not refused to redeem its circulating notes, when legally presented, in the lawful money of the United States, shall make an order enjoining the Comptroller, and any receiver acting under his direction, from all further proceedings on account of such alleged refusal.

Expense of protest, receivership, &c., how paid.

SEC. 51. *And be it further enacted*, That all fees for protesting the notes issued by any such banking association shall be paid by the person procuring the protest to be made, and such banking association shall be liable therefor; but no part of the bonds pledged by such banking association, as aforesaid, shall be applied to the payment of such fees. And all expenses of any preliminary or other examinations into the condition of any association shall be paid by such association; and all expenses of any receivership shall be paid out of the assets of such association before distribution of the proceeds thereof.

Transfer of property of insolvent banks, and other acts giving preference, void.

SEC. 52. *And be it further enacted*, That all transfer of the notes, bonds, bills of exchange, and other evidences of debt owing to any association, or of deposits to its credit; all assignments of mortgages, sureties on real estate, or of judgments or decrees in its favor; all deposits of money, bullion, or other valuable thing for its use, or for the use of any of its shareholders or creditors; and all payments of money to either, made after the commission of an act of insolvency, or in contemplation thereof, with a view to prevent the application of its assets in the manner prescribed by this act, or with a view to the preference of one creditor to another, except in payment of its circulating notes, shall be utterly null and void.

## VIOLATION OF LAW BY DIRECTORS

Violation of law by directors to forfeit rights, &c., of bank, and directors liable for damages.

SEC. 53. *And be it further enacted*, That if the directors of any association shall knowingly violate, or knowingly permit any of the officers, agents, or servants of the association to violate, any of the provisions of this act, all the rights, privileges, and franchises of the association derived from this act shall be thereby forfeited. Such violation shall, however, be determined and adjudged by a proper circuit, district, or territorial court of the United States, in a suit brought for that purpose by the Comptroller of the Currency, in his own name, before the association shall be declared dissolved. And in cases of such violation, every director who participated in or assented to the same shall be held liable in his personal and individual capacity for all damages which the association, its shareholders, or any other person, shall have sustained in consequence of such violation.

### BANK EXAMINERS.

Bank examiners, their duty and pay.

SEC. 54. *And be it further enacted,* That the Comptroller of the Currency, with the approbation of the Secretary of the Treasury, as often as shall be deemed necessary or proper, shall appoint a suitable person or persons to make an examination of the affairs of every banking association, which person shall not be a director or other officer in any association whose affairs he shall be appointed to examine, and who shall have power to make a thorough examination into all the affairs of the association, and, in doing so, to examine any of the officers and agents thereof on oath; and shall make a full and detailed report of the condition of the association to the Comptroller. And the association shall not be subject to any other visitorial powers than such as are authorized by this act, except such as are vested in the several courts of law and chancery. And every person appointed to make such examination shall receive for his services at the rate of five dollars for each day by him employed in such examination, and two dollars for every twenty-five miles he shall necessarily travel in the performance of his duty, which shall be paid by the association by him examined.

### MISDEMEANORS OF OFFICERS.

Embezzlement, willful misapplication of funds, and other misdemeanors, how punished.

SEC. 55. *And be it further enacted,* That every president, director, cashier, teller, clerk, or agent of any association,[26]

26. The act of April 6, 1869, chapter 11, provides for the punishment of persons aiding or abetting officers or agents in doing any of the acts enumer-

who shall embezzle, abstract, or willfully misapply any of the moneys, funds, or credits of the association, or shall, without authority from the directors, issue or put in circulation any of the notes of the association, or shall, without such authority, issue or put forth any certificate of deposit, draw any order or bill of exchange, make any acceptance, assign any note, bond, draft, bill of exchange, mortgage, judgment, or decree, or shall make any false entry in any book, report, or statement of the association, with intent, in either case, to injure or defraud the association or any other company, body politic, or corporate, or any individual person, or to deceive any officer of the association, or any agent appointed to examine the affairs of any such association, shall be deemed guilty of a misdemeanor, and upon conviction thereof shall be punished by imprisonment not less than five nor more than ten years.

SUITS AGAINST BANKS.

Certain suits to be conducted by U. S. attorney, &c.

SEC. 56. *And be it further enacted*, That all suits and proceedings arising out of the provisions of this act, in which the United States or its officers or agents shall be parties, shall be conducted by the district attorneys of the several districts,[27] under the direction and supervision of the Solicitor of the Treasury.

Jurisdiction of suits against banks.

SEC. 57. *And be it further enacted*, That suits, actions, and proceedings against[28] any association under this act, may be had in any circuit, district, or territorial court of the United States held within the district in which such association may be established,[29] or in any State, county,

---

ated in this section. And the act of July 8, 1870, chapter 226, declares to what officers and what banks the section and the amendment thereto shall apply.

27. The requirement of this section that all suits, &c., under this act shall be conducted by the district attorneys of the several districts is merely directory, and suits may be conducted by private counsel. (*Kennedy* v. *Gibson et al.*, 8 *Wallace*, 504.)

28. Under this section suits may be brought *by* as well as *against* national banks in the courts therein mentioned. The omission of the word "by" is decided to be accidental. (*Kennedy* v. *Gibson et al.*, 8 *Wallace*, 506.)

29. The Supreme Judicial Court of Massachusetts has decided that a na-

or municipal court in the county or city in which said association is located, having jurisdiction in similar cases: *Provided, however*,[30] That all proceedings to enjoin the Comptroller under this act shall be had in a circuit, district, or territorial court of the United States, held in the district in which the association is located.

MUTILATION OF NOTES.

Mutilating notes and other evidences of debts, punishable.

SEC. 58. *And be it further enacted*, That every person who shall mutilate, cut, deface, disfigure, or perforate with holes, or shall unite or cement together, or do any other thing to any bank bill, draft, note, or other evidence of debt, issued by any such association, or shall cause or procure the same to be done, with intent to render such bank bill, draft, note, or other evidence of debt unfit to be reissued by said association, shall, upon conviction, forfeit fifty dollars to the association who shall be injured thereby, to be recovered by action in any court having jurisdiction.

FORGERY, CONTERFEITING, PASSING COUNTERFEIT NOTES, MAKING FALSE PLATES, AND OTHER OFFENSES.

Forgery, counterfeiting notes, passing forged notes, &c.

SEC. 59. *And be it further enacted*, That if any person shall falsely make, forge, or counterfeit, or cause or procure to be made, forged, or counterfeited, or willingly aid or assist in falsely making, forging, or counterfeiting, any note in imitation of, or purporting to be in imitation of, the circulating notes issued under the provisions of this act, or shall pass, utter, or publish, or attempt to pass, utter, or publish any false, forged, or counterfeited note, purporting to be issued by any association doing a banking business under the provisions of this act, knowing the same to be

---

tional bank can be sued in a State court only in the county or city in which it is established. The Supreme Court of New York has decided otherwise, and holds that a national bank may be sued even in a *State* other than that in which it is located. (*Crocker* v. *Marine National Bank of New York*, 101 *Mass.*, 240; *Cooke* v. *State National Bank of Boston*, 50 *Barbour*, 339.)

30. This proviso does not give to United States circuit courts jurisdiction of a suit in equity to interfere with the United States Treasurer or Comptroller of the Currency in their duties respecting bonds deposited for the security of notes, and those courts have no such jurisdiction. (*Van Antwerp* v. *Hulburd*, 7 *Blatchford C. C. R.*, 426; *Same*, 8 *Blatchford C. C. R.*, 282.)

falsely made, forged, or counterfeited, or shall falsely alter, or cause or procure to be falsely altered, or willingly aid or assist in falsely altering, any such circulating notes, issued as aforesaid, or shall pass, utter, or publish, or attempt to pass, utter, or publish, as true, any falsely altered or spurious circulating note issued, or purporting to have been issued, as aforesaid, knowing the same to be falsely altered or spurious, every such person shall be deemed and adjudged guilty of felony, and being thereof convicted by due course of law shall be sentenced to be imprisoned and kept at hard labor for a period of not less than five years nor more than fifteen years, and fined in a sum not exceeding one thousand dollars.

**Making, procuring, or having false plates, dies, &c.**

SEC. 60. *And be it further enacted*, That if any person shall make or engrave, or cause or procure to be made or engraved, or shall have in his custody or possession, any plate, die, or block after the similitude of any plate, die, or block from which any circulating notes issued as aforesaid shall have been prepared or printed, with intent to use such plate, die, or block, or cause or suffer the same to be used, in forging or counterfeiting any of the notes issued as aforesaid, or shall have in his custody or possession any blank note or notes engraved and printed after the similitude of any notes issued as aforesaid, with intent to use such blanks, or cause or suffer the same to be used in forging or counterfeiting any of the notes issued as aforesaid, or shall have in his custody or possession any paper adapted to the making of such notes, and similar to the paper upon which any such notes shall have been issued, with intent to use such paper, or cause or suffer the same to be used, in forging or counterfeiting any of the notes issued as aforesaid, every such person, being thereof convicted by due course of law, shall be sentenced to be imprisoned and kept to hard labor for a term not less than five or more than fifteen years, and fined in a sum not exceeding one thousand dollars.

Having false notes,

—or paper adapted to making notes.

## REPORT OF COMPTROLLER.

Comptroller's report, when to be made and what to contain.

SEC. 61. *And be it further enacted*, That it shall be the duty of the Comptroller of the Currency to report annually to Congress at the commencement of its session—

*First.* A summary of the state and condition of every association from whom reports have been received the preceding year, at the several dates to which such reports refer, with an abstract of the whole amount of banking capital returned by them, of the whole amount of their debts and liabilities, the amount of circulating notes outstanding, and the total amount of means and resources, specifying the amount of lawful money held by them at the times of their several returns, and such other information in relation to said association as in his judgment may be useful.

*Second.* A statement of the associations whose business has been closed during the year, with the amount of their circulation redeemed and the amount outstanding.

*Third.* Any amendment to the laws relative to banking by which the system may be improved, and the security of the holders of its notes and other creditors may be increased.

*Fourth.* The names and compensation of the clerks employed by him, and the whole amount of the expenses of the banking department during the year. And such report shall be made by or before the first day of December in each year, and the usual number of copies for the use of the Senate and House, and one thousand copies for the use of the Department, shall be printed by the Public Printer and in readiness for distribution at the first meeting of Congress.

FORMER ACT REPEALED.

Repeal of act of February 25, 1863.

SEC. 62. *And be it further enacted,* That the act entitled "An act to provide a national currency, secured by a pledge of United States stocks, and to provide for the circulation and redemption thereof," approved February twenty-fifth, eighteen hundred and sixty-three, is hereby repealed: *Provided,* That such repeal shall not affect any appointments made, acts done, or proceedings had, or the organization, acts, or proceedings of any association organized or in the process of organization under the act aforesaid: *And provided, also,* That all such associations so organized or in process of organization shall enjoy all the rights and privileges granted, and be subject to all the duties, liabilities, and restrictions imposed by this act, and with the approval

Saving clause.

Privileges of this act conferred on banks organized under former act.

of the Comptroller of the Currency, in lieu of the name specified in their respective organization certificates, may take any other name preferred by them and duly certified to the Comptroller, without prejudice to any right acquired under this act, or under the act hereby repealed; but no such change shall be made after six months from the passage of this act: *Provided, also*, That the circulation issued or to be issued by such association shall be considered as a part of the circulation provided for in this act.

LIABILITY OF EXECUTORS, TRUSTEES, &C.

Estates held by executors, &c., to be liable.

SEC. 63. *And be it further enacted*, That persons holding stock as executors, administrators, guardians, and trustees, shall not be personally subject to any liabilities as stockholders; but the estates and funds in their hands shall be liable in like manner and to the same extent as the testator, intestate, ward, or person interested in said trust funds would be if they were respectively living and competent to act and hold the stock in their own names.

AMENDMENT AND REPEAL OF ACT.

Congress may repeal or alter act.

SEC. 64. *And be it further enacted*, That Congress may at any time amend, alter, or repeal this act.

*Approved June* 3, 1864.

ACT OF JUNE 30, 1864, CHAPTER 173.

AN ACT TO PROVIDE INTERNAL REVENUE FOR THE SUPPORT OF THE GOVERNMENT, TO PAY INTEREST ON THE PUBLIC DEBT, AND FOR OTHER PURPOSES.

TAXES ON BANKS AND BANKERS, OTHER THAN NATIONAL BANKS.

Tax on average deposits.

SEC. 110. *And be it further enacted*, That there shall be levied, collected, and paid a tax of one twenty-fourth of one per centum each month[31] upon the average amount of the deposits of money, subject to payment by check or draft, or represented by certificates of deposit or otherwise, whether

31. Taxes imposed by this section are now payable semi-annually, on the first day of January and July, by the act of June 6, 1872, chapter 315, section 37. (*See page* 158.)

payable on demand or at some future day, with any person, bank, association, company, or corporation engaged in the business of banking;

And a tax of one twenty-fourth of one per centum each month,[31] as aforesaid, upon the capital of any bank, association, company, or corporation, and on the capital employed[32] by any person in the business of banking beyond the average amount invested in United States bonds. On capital.

And a tax of one-twelfth of one per centum each month[31] upon the average amount of circulation issued by any bank, association, corporation, company, or person, including as circulation all certified checks and all notes and other obligations calculated or intended to circulate or to be used as money, but not including that in the vault of the bank, or redeemed and on deposit for said bank; and an additional tax of one-sixth of one per centum, each month, upon the average amount of such circulation, issued as aforesaid, beyond the amount of ninety per centum of the capital of any such bank, association, corporation, company, or person. On circulation.

And a true and accurate return of the amount of circulation, of deposit, and of capital, as aforesaid, and of the amount of notes of persons, State banks, or State banking associations, paid out by them for the previous month, shall be made and rendered monthly by each of such banks, associations, corporations, companies, or persons, to the assessor of the district in which any such bank, association, corporation, or company may be located, or in which such person has his place of business, with a declaration annexed thereto, and the oath or affirmation of such person, or of the president or cashier of such bank, association, corporation, or company, in such form and manner as may be prescribed by the Commissioner of Internal Revenue, that the same contains a true and faithful statement of the amounts subject to tax as aforesaid; and for any refusal or neglect to make Returns to be made.

---

31. See note on preceding page.

32. The act of June 6, 1872, chapter 315, section 37, provides that "capital employed" shall not include money borrowed or received from day to day, in the usual course of banking business, from any person not a partner of, or interested in, the said bank, association, or firm.

or to render return and payment, any such bank, association, corporation, company, or person so in default shall be subject to and pay a penalty of two hundred dollars, besides the additional penalty and forfeitures in other cases provided by law; and the amount of circulation, deposit, capital, and notes of persons, State banks, and banking associations, paid out as aforesaid, in default of the proper return, shall be estimated by the assessor or assistant assessor of the district as aforesaid upon the best information he can obtain; and every such penalty may be recovered for the use of the United States in any court of competent jurisdiction.

On banks with branches.

And in the case of banks with branches, the tax herein provided for shall be assessed upon the circulation of each branch severally, and the amount of capital of each branch shall be considered to be the amount allotted to such branch;

Repeal of former provisions.

And so much of an act entitled "An act to provide ways and means for the support of the Government," approved March three, eighteen hundred and sixty-three, as imposes any tax on banks, their circulation, capital, or deposits, other than is herein provided, is hereby repealed:

Act not to apply to national banks.

*Provided*, That this section shall not apply to associations which are taxed under and by virtue of the act "to provide a national currency secured by a pledge of United States bonds, and to provide for the circulation and redemption thereof." And the deposits in associations or companies known as provident associations, savings banks, savings funds, or savings institutions, having no capital stock, and doing no other business than receiving deposits to be loaned or invested for the sole benefit of the parties making such deposits, without profit or compensation to the association or company, shall be exempt from tax on so much of their deposits as they have invested in securities of the United States, and on all deposits less than five hundred dollars[33] made in the name of any one person; and the returns required to be made by such provident institutions and savings banks after July, eighteen hundred

Savings banks, &c., how taxed.

33. The exemption is extended to two thousand dollars by the act of June 6, 1872, chapter 315, section 37.

and sixty-six, shall be made on the first Monday of January and July of each year, in such form and manner as may be prescribed by the Commissioner of Internal Revenue. [*As amended by the act of July* 13, 1866, *chapter* 184, § 9.]

### ACT OF MARCH 3, 1865, CHAPTER 78.

AN ACT TO AMEND AN ACT ENTITLED "AN ACT TO PROVIDE INTERNAL REVENUE TO SUPPORT THE GOVERNMENT, TO PAY INTEREST ON THE PUBLIC DEBT, AND FOR OTHER PURPOSES," APPROVED JUNE 30, 1864.

#### TAX ON NOTES OF STATE BANKS, &C.

Ten per cent. tax on notes of persons and State banks used for circulation.

SEC. 6. *And be it further enacted*, That every national banking association, State bank, or State banking association, shall pay a tax of ten per centum [34] on the amount of notes of any person, State bank, or State banking association, used for circulation and paid out by them after the first day of August, eighteen hundred and sixty-six, and such tax shall be assessed and paid in such manner as shall be prescribed by the Commissioner of Internal Revenue. [*As amended by act of July* 13, 1866, *chapter* 184, § 9 *bis*.]

#### CONVERSION OF STATE BANKS WITH BRANCHES.

State banks with branches may become national banks and retain branches.

SEC. 7. * * * *Provided*, That it shall be lawful for any bank or banking association organized under State laws, and having branches, the capital being joint and assigned to and used by the mother bank and branches in

34. This section, taxing banks ten per cent. on the amount of notes of State banks paid out by them, is held to be constitutional by the Supreme Court of the United States. (*Veazie Bank* v. *Fenno*, 8 *Wallace*, 534.)

The tax applies to the notes which a bank pays out *of its own issue* as well as of the issue of other banks. (*Official Opinion of Attorney General Williams*, 1872; *Veazie Bank* v. *Fenno*, 8 *Wallace*, 534.)

The act of March 26, 1867, chapter 8, section 2, lays a tax of ten per cent. on the notes of any town, city, or municipal corporation paid out for circulation. (*See page* 148.)

And the act of July 17, 1862, chapter 196, section 2, makes it a penal offence to make, issue, circulate, or pay any note, check, memorandum, token, or other obligation for a less sum than one dollar, intended to circulate as money, or to be received or used in lieu of lawful money. (*See page* 45.)

definite proportions, to become a national banking association in conformity with existing laws, and to retain and keep in operation its branches, or such one or more of them as it may elect to retain; the amount of the circulation redeemable at the mother bank and each branch to be regulated by the amount of capital assigned to and used by each. * * * * *

CAPITAL OF BANKS CONVERTED.

Capital of State banks converted.

SEC. 14. *And be it further enacted*, That the capital of any State bank or banking association, which has ceased or shall cease to exist, or which has been or shall be converted into a national bank, shall be assumed to be the capital as it existed immediately before such bank ceased to exist or was converted as aforesaid.

CIRCULATION, WHEN NOT TAXABLE.

Circulation not taxable when it does not exceed five per cent. of capital.

And whenever the outstanding circulation of any bank, association, corporation, company, or person shall be reduced to an amount not exceeding five per centum of the chartered or declared capital existing at the time the same was issued, said circulation shall be free from taxation;[35] and whenever any bank which has ceased to issue notes for circulation shall deposit in the Treasury of the United States, in lawful money, the amount of its outstanding circulation, to be redeemed at par, under such regulations as the Secretary of the Treasury shall prescribe, it shall be exempt from any tax upon such circulation;

TAX ON STATE BANKS AFTER CONVERSION.

National banks converted from State banks—

And whenever any State bank or banking association has been converted into a national banking association, and such

35. This provision relieves banks which are withdrawing their circulation or have reduced it to five per cent. of their capital, for any reason, from the tax imposed on national banks by section 41 of the act of June 3, 1864, (*see page* 125,) and on State banks by section 110 of the act of June 30, 1864, as amended by the act of July 13, 1866, (*see page* 142,) but not from the ten per cent. tax imposed on amount of notes of any State bank or banking association, *whether notes of their own* or those of other banks, by section 6 of the act of March 3, 1865, as amended by act of July 13, 1866, section 9. (*See page* 145.) (*Official Opinion of Attorney General Williams*, 1872,)

national banking association has assumed the liabilities of such State bank or banking association, including the redemption of its bills, by any agreement or understanding whatever with the representatives of such State bank or banking association, such national banking association shall be held to make the required return and payment on the circulation outstanding, so long as such circulation shall exceed five per centum of the capital before such conversion of such State bank or banking association. [*As amended by act of July* 13, 1866, *chapter* 184, § 9 *bis.*]

—to pay tax due from latter and make returns, &c.

### ACT OF MARCH 2, 1867, CHAPTER 194.

AN ACT TO PROVIDE WAYS AND MEANS FOR THE PAYMENT OF COMPOUND-INTEREST NOTES.

*Be it enacted by the Senate and House of Representatives of the United States of America in Congress assembled*, That for the purpose of redeeming and retiring any compound-interest notes outstanding, the Secretary of the Treasury is hereby authorized and directed to issue temporary loan certificates,[36] in the manner prescribed by section four of the act entitled "An act to authorize the issue of United States notes and for the redemption or funding thereof, and for funding the floating debt of the United States," approved February twenty-fifth, eighteen hundred and sixty-two, bearing interest at a rate not exceeding three per centum per annum, principal and interest payable in lawful money on demand;

Temporary loan or three per cent. certificates.

And said certificates of temporary loan may constitute and be held, by any national bank holding or owning the same, as a part of the reserve provided for in sections thirty-one and thirty-two of the act entitled "An act to provide a national currency, secured by a pledge of United States bonds, and to provide for the circulation and redemption

May be held by banks as part of their reserves.

36. By the act of July 25, 1868, chapter 237, the amount of temporary loan certificates to be issued was increased to seventy-five millions dollars, and by the act of July 12, 1870, chapter 252, section 2, they are all required to be called in for payment as fast as additional currency notes are issued under that act. When called in for payment they cease to bear interest, and can no longer be held as part of the bank reserves. (*See page* 28.)

thereof," approved June three, eighteen hundred and sixty-four: *Provided*, That not less than two-fifths of the entire reserve of such bank shall consist of lawful money of the United States: *And provided further*, That the amount of such temporary certificates at any time outstanding shall not exceed fifty millions of dollars.

*Approved, March* 2, 1867.

### ACT OF MARCH 26, 1867, CHAPTER 8.

AN ACT TO EXEMPT WRAPPING PAPER, MADE FROM WOOD OR CORNSTALKS, FROM INTERNAL TAX, AND FOR OTHER PURPOSES.

Banks and bankers to pay ten per cent. tax on amount of notes of towns, cities, and municipal corporations paid out by them.

SEC. 2. *And be it further enacted*, That every national banking association, State bank, or banker, or association shall pay a tax of ten per centum on the amount of notes of any town, city, or municipal corporation paid out by them after the first day of May, anno Domini eighteen hundred and sixty-seven, to be collected in the mode and manner in which the tax on the notes of State banks is collected.

*Approved, March* 26, 1867.

### ACT OF FEBRUARY 10, 1868, CHAPTER 7.

AN ACT IN RELATION TO TAXING SHARES IN NATIONAL BANKS.

Where shares of banks may be taxed.

*Be it enacted by the Senate and House of Representatives of the United States of America in Congress assembled*, That the words "place where the bank is located, and not elsewhere," in section forty-one of the "act to provide a national currency," approved June third, eighteen hundred and sixty-four, shall be construed and held to mean the State within which the bank is located; and the Legislature of each State may determine and direct the manner and place of taxing all the shares of national banks located within said State, subject to the restriction that the taxation shall not be at a greater rate than is assessed upon any other moneyed capital in the hands of individual citizens of such State: *And provided always*, That the shares of any national bank owned by non-residents of any State shall be

Shares of non-residents.

taxed in the city or town where said bank is located, and not elsewhere.

*Approved, February* 10, 1868.

## ACT OF FEBRUARY 19, 1869, CHAPTER 32.

### AN ACT TO PREVENT LOANING MONEY UPON UNITED STATES NOTES.

*Be it enacted by the Senate and House of Representatives of the United States of America in Congress assembled,* That no national banking association shall hereafter offer or receive United States notes or national bank notes as security or as collateral security for any loan of money, or for a consideration shall agree to withhold the same from use, or shall offer or receive the custody or promise of custody of such notes as security, or as collateral security, or consideration for any loan of money; and any national banking association offending against the provisions of this act shall be deemed guilty of a misdemeanor, and, upon conviction thereof in any United States court having jurisdiction shall be punished by a fine not exceeding one thousand dollars, and by a further sum equal to one-third of the money so loaned; and the officer or officers of said bank who shall make such loan or loans shall be liable for a further sum equal to one-quarter of the money so loaned; and the prosecution of such offenders shall be commenced and conducted as provided for the punishment of offenses in an act to provide a national currency, approved June third, eighteen hundred and sixty-four, and the fine or penalty so recovered shall be for the benefit of the party bringing such suit.

Offering or receiving U. S. notes as security for loans, or agreeing to withhold same from use—how punished.

*Approved, February* 19, 1869.

## ACT OF MARCH 3, 1869, CHAPTER 130.

### AN ACT REGULATING THE REPORTS OF NATIONAL BANKING ASSOCIATIONS.

*Be it enacted by the Senate and House of Representatives of the United States of America in Congress assembled,* That in lieu of all reports required by section thirty-four of the national currency act, every association shall make to the

Banks to make not less than five reports annually

Comptroller of the Currency not less than five reports during each and every year, according to the form which may be prescribed by him, verified by the oath or affirmation of the president or cashier of such association, and attested by

Details of reports.

the signature of at least three of the directors; which report shall exhibit, in detail and under appropriate heads, the resources and liabilities of the association at the close of

Reports to be sent to the Comptroller;

business on any past day to be by him specified, and shall transmit such report to the Comptroller within five days after the receipt of a request or requisition therefor from him; and the report of each association above required, in the same form in which it is made to the Comptroller, shall

—also to be published.

be published in a newspaper published in the place where such association is established, or if there be no newspaper in the place, then in the one published nearest thereto in the same county, at the expense of the association; and such proof of publication shall be furnished as may be required by the Comptroller.

Special reports.

And the Comptroller shall have power to call for special reports from any particular association whenever in his judgment the same shall be necessary in order to a full and complete knowledge of its condition.

Penalties.

Any association failing to make and transmit any such report shall be subject to a penalty of one hundred dollars for each day after five days that such bank shall delay to make and transmit any report as aforesaid; and in case any association shall delay or refuse to pay the penalty herein imposed when the same shall be assessed by the Comptroller of the Currency, the amount of such penalty may be retained by the Treasurer of the United States, upon the order of the Comptroller of the Currency, out of the interest, as it may become due to the association, on the bonds deposited with him to secure circulation; and all sums of money collected for penalties under this section shall be paid into the Treasury of the United States.

Additional reports of dividends and net earnings.

SEC. 2. *And be it further enacted*, That, in addition to said reports, each national banking association shall report to the Comptroller of the Currency the amount of each dividend declared by said association, and the amount of net earnings in excess of said dividends, which report shall be made within ten days after the declaration of each dividend, and attested by the oath of the president or cashier of said association, and a failure to comply with the provisions of this section shall subject such association to the penalties provided in the foregoing section.

*Approved, March* 3, 1869.

### ACT OF MARCH 3, 1869, CHAPTER 135.

AN ACT IN REFERENCE TO CERTIFYING CHECKS BY NATIONAL BANKS.

*Be it enacted by the Senate and House of Representatives of the United States of America in Congress assembled*, That it shall be unlawful for any officer, clerk, or agent of any national bank to certify any check drawn upon said bank unless the person or company drawing said check shall have on deposit in said bank at the time such check is certified an amount of money equal to the amount specified in such check; and any check so certified by duly authorized officers shall be a good and valid obligation against such bank; and any officer, clerk, or agent of any national bank violating the provisions of this act shall subject such bank to the liabilities and proceedings on the part of the Comptroller as provided for in section fifty of the national banking law, approved June third, eighteen hundred and sixty-four.

Checks not to be certified unless drawn against actual deposits.

Certified checks to be valid. Penalty for violation of law.

*Approved, March* 3, 1869.

### ACT OF APRIL 6, 1869, CHAPTER 11.

AN ACT TO AMEND AN ACT ENTITLED "AN ACT TO PROVIDE A NATIONAL CURRENCY SECURED BY A PLEDGE OF UNITED STATES BONDS, AND TO PROVIDE FOR THE CIRCULATION AND REDEMPTION THEREOF," APPROVED JUNE THIRD, EIGHTEEN HUNDRED AND SIXTY-FOUR, BY EXTENDING CERTAIN PENALTIES TO ACCESSORIES.

*Be it enacted by the Senate and House of Representatives of the United States of America in Congress assembled*, That every person who shall aid or abet any officer or agent of any association in doing any of the acts enumerated in section fifty-five of an act entitled "An act to provide a national

Aiding or abetting officers &c. of banks, in embezzlement of funds and other unlawful acts, punishable.

currency secured by a pledge of United States bonds, and to provide for the circulation and redemption thereof," approved June third, eighteen hundred and sixty-four, with intent to defraud or deceive, shall be liable to the same punishment therein provided for the principal.

*Approved, April* 6, 1869.

### ACT OF JULY 8, 1870, CHAPTER 226.

AN ACT TO DECLARE THE CONSTRUCTION OF SECTION FIFTY-FIVE OF AN ACT ENTITLED "AN ACT TO PROVIDE A NATIONAL CURRENCY SECURED BY A PLEDGE OF UNITED STATES BONDS, AND TO PROVIDE FOR THE CIRCULATION AND REDEMPTION THEREOF," APPROVED JUNE THREE, EIGHTEEN HUNDRED AND SIXTY-FOUR, AND THE ACTS AMENDATORY THEREOF AND TO AMEND THE SAME.

To what officers penalty against embezzlement shall apply.

*Be it enacted by the Senate and House of Representatives of the United States of America in Congress assembled*, That section fifty-five of the act entitled "An act to provide a national currency secured by a pledge of United States bonds, and to provide for the circulation and redemption thereof," approved June three, eighteen hundred and sixty-four, and all acts amendatory of said section, shall be construed to apply to every president, director, cashier, teller, clerk, or agent of any banking association, whether organized under the aforesaid act or under the act entitled "An act to provide a national currency secured by a pledge of United States bonds, and to provide for the circulation and redemption thereof," approved February twenty-five, eighteen hundred and sixty-three.

*Approved, July* 8, 1870.

### ACT OF JULY 12, 1870, CHAPTER 252.

AN ACT TO PROVIDE FOR THE REDEMPTION OF THE THREE PER CENT. TEMPORARY LOAN CERTIFICATES, AND FOR AN INCREASE OF NATIONAL BANK NOTES.

Additional circulation authorized—$54,000,000.

*Be it enacted by the Senate and House of Representatives of the United States of America in Congress assembled*, That fifty-four millions of dollars in notes for circulation may be issued to national banking associations, in addition to the three hundred millions of dollars authorized by the twenty-second section of the "Act to provide a national currency secured by a pledge of United States bonds, and to provide for the circulation and redemption thereof," approved June three, eighteen hundred and sixty-four;

And the amount of notes so provided shall be furnished to banking associations organized or to be organized in those States and Territories having less than their proportion under the apportionment contemplated by the provisions of the "Act to amend an act to provide a national currency, secured by a pledge of United States bonds, and to provide for the circulation and redemption thereof," approved March three, eighteen hundred and sixty-five, and the bonds deposited with the Treasurer of the United States, to secure the additional circulating notes herein authorized, shall be of any description of bonds of the United States bearing interest in coin, but a new apportionment of the increased circulation herein provided for shall be made as soon as practicable, based upon the census of eighteen hundred and seventy: *Provided*, That if applications for the circulation herein authorized shall not be made within one year after the passage of this act by banking associations organized or to be organized in States having less than their proportion, it shall be lawful for the Comptroller of the Currency to issue such circulation to banking associations applying for the same in other States or Territories having less than their proportion, giving the preference to such as have the greatest deficiency; **How distributed.**

*And provided further*, That no banking association hereafter organized shall have a circulation in excess of five hundred thousand dollars. **Circulation currency banks not to exceed $500,000 each.**

SEC. 2. *And be it further enacted*, That at the end of each month after the passage of this act it shall be the duty of the Comptroller of the Currency to report to the Secretary of the Treasury the amount of circulating notes issued, under the provisions of the preceding section, to national banking associations during the previous month; **Comptroller to report, monthly, amount of issue.**

Whereupon the Secretary of the Treasury shall redeem and cancel an amount of the three per centum temporary **Three per cent. certificates to be** redeemed and canceled.

loan certificates issued under the acts of March two, eighteen hundred and sixty-seven, and July twenty-five, eighteen hundred and sixty-eight, not less than the amount of circulating notes so reported, and may, if necessary, in order to procure the presentation of such temporary loan certificates for redemption, give notice to the holders thereof, by publication or otherwise, that certain of said certificates (which shall be designated by number, date, and amount) shall cease to bear interest from and after a day to be designated in such notice, and that the certificates so designated shall no longer be available as any portion of the lawful money reserve in possession of any national banking association, and after the day designated in such notice no interest shall be paid on such certificates, and they shall not thereafter be counted as a part of the reserve of any banking association.

Notice to holders of three per cent. certificates.

No longer to be held as part of the bank reserves.

NATIONAL GOLD BANKS AND GOLD NOTES.

Banks may have circulation redeemable in gold coin.

SEC. 3. *And be it further enacted*, That upon the deposit of any United States bonds, bearing interest payable in gold, with the Treasurer of the United States, in the manner prescribed in the nineteenth and twentieth sections of the national currency act, it shall be lawful for the Comptroller of the Currency to issue to the association making the same circulating notes of different denominations, not less than five dollars, not exceeding in amount eighty per centum of the par value of the bonds deposited, which notes shall bear upon their face the promise of the association to which they are issued to pay them, upon presentation at the office of the association, in gold coin of the United States, and shall be redeemable upon such presentation in such coin: *Provided*, That no banking association organized under this section shall have a circulation in excess of one million of dollars.

Circulation of gold banks not to exceed $1,000,000 each.

Reserve of 25 per cent. of circulation to be kept in coin.

SEC. 4. *And be it further enacted*, That every national banking association formed under the provisions of the preceding section of this act shall at all times keep on hand not less than twenty-five per centum of its outstanding circulation in gold or silver coin of the United States, and shall receive at par in the payment of debts the gold notes of every other such banking association which at the time of such payments shall be redeeming its circulating notes in gold coin of the United States.

Gold notes receivable at par by all gold banks.

SEC. 5. *And be it further enacted*, That every association organized for the purpose of issuing gold notes as provided in this act, shall be subject to all the requirements and provisions of the national currency act, except the first clause of section twenty-two, which limits the circulation of national banking associations to three hundred millions of dollars; the first clause of section thirty-two, which, taken in connection with the preceding section, would require national banking associations organized in the city of San Francisco to redeem their circulating notes at par in the city of New York; and the last clause of section thirty-two, which requires every national banking association to receive in payment of debts the notes of every other national banking association at par: *Provided*, That in applying the provisions and requirements of said act to the banking associations herein provided for, the terms "lawful money," and "lawful money of the United States," shall be held and construed to mean gold or silver coin of the United States.

National gold banks subject to general banking law with certain exceptions

DISTRIBUTION OF CIRCULATION OF CURRENCY BANKS AMONG STATES.

SEC. 6. *And be it further enacted*, That to secure a more equitable distribution of the national banking currency there may be issued circulating notes to banking associations organized in States and Territories having less than their proportion as herein set forth. And the amount of circulation in this section authorized shall, under the direction of the Secretary of the Treasury, as it may be required for this purpose, be withdrawn, as herein provided, from banking associations organized in States having a circulation exceeding that provided for by the act entitled "An act to amend an act entitled 'An act to provide for a national banking currency secured by pledge of United States bonds, and to provide for the circulation and redemption thereof,'" approved March three, eighteen hundred and

Redistribution of circulation to extent of $25,000,000 may be made to banks in States, &c., not having their proportion, and withdrawn from others.

sixty-five, but the amount so withdrawn shall not exceed twenty-five million dollars.

How reduction shall be made from States having an excess.

The Comptroller of the Currency shall, under the direction of the Secretary of the Treasury, make a statement showing the amount of circulation in each State and Territory, and the amount to be retired by each banking association in accordance with this section, and shall, when such redistribution of circulation is required, make a requisition for such amount upon such banks, commencing with the banks having a circulation exceeding one million of dollars in States having an excess of circulation, and withdrawing their circulation in excess of one million of dollars, and then proceeding pro rata with other banks having a circulation exceeding three hundred thousand dollars in States having the largest excess of circulation, and reducing the circulation of such banks in States having the greatest proportion in excess, leaving undisturbed the banks in States having a smaller proportion, until those in greater excess have been reduced to the same grade, and continuing thus to make the reduction provided for by this act until the full amount of twenty-five millions, herein provided for, shall be withdrawn; and the circulation so withdrawn shall be distributed among the States and Territories having less than their proportion, so as to equalize the same. And it shall be the duty of the Comptroller of the Currency, under the direction of the Secretary of the Treasury, forthwith to make a requisition for the amount thereof upon the banks above indicated as herein prescribed.

If banks fail to return circulation when required, their bonds to be sold and notes redeemed.

And upon failure of such associations, or any of them, to return the amount so required within one year, it shall be the duty of the Comptroller of the Currency to sell at public auction, having given twenty days' notice thereof in one daily newspaper printed in Washington and one in New York city, an amount of bonds deposited by said association, as security for said circulation, equal to the circulation to be withdrawn from said association and not returned in compliance with such requisition; and the Comptroller of the Currency shall with the proceeds redeem so many of the notes of said banking association, as they come into the

Treasury, as will equal the amount required and not so returned, and shall pay the balance, if any, to such banking association:

*Provided*, That no circulation shall be withdrawn under the provisions of this section until after the fifty-four millions granted in the first section shall have been taken up.

SEC. 7. *And be it further enacted*, That after the expiration of six months from the passage of this act any banking association located in any State having more than its proportion of circulation may be removed to any State having less than its proportion of circulation, under such rules and regulations as the Comptroller of the Currency, with the approval of the Secretary of the Treasury, may require: *Provided*, That the amount of the issue of said banks shall not be deducted from the amount of new issue provided for in this act.

Banks in States having excess of circulation may remove to States having less than their proportion.

*Approved, July* 12, 1870

## ACT OF JULY 14, 1870, CHAPTER 257.

### AN ACT TO REQUIRE NATIONAL BANKS GOING INTO LIQUIDATION TO RETIRE THEIR CIRCULATING NOTES.

*Be it enacted by the Senate and House of Representatives of the United States of America in Congress assembled*, That every bank that has heretofore gone into liquidation under the provisions of section forty-two of the national currency act, shall be required to deposit lawful money of the United States for its outstanding circulation within sixty days from the date of the passage of this act.

Banks in liquidation to deposit money to redeem outstanding circulation—

And every bank that may hereafter go into liquidation shall be required to deposit lawful money of the United States for its outstanding circulation within six months from the date of the vote to go into liquidation; whereupon the bonds pledged as security for such circulation shall be surrendered to the association making such deposit.

—within six months from date of vote to go into liquidation—

And if any bank shall fail to make the deposit and take up its bonds for thirty days after the expiration of the time specified, the Comptroller of the Currency shall have power to sell the bonds pledged for the circulation of said bank

—otherwise bonds may be sold.

at public auction in New York city, and after providing for the redemption and cancellation of said circulation, and the necessary expenses of the sale, to pay over any balance remaining from the proceeds to the bank or its legal representative:

Certain banks exempt from above provisions but to report assets and liabilities.

*Provided*, That banks which are winding up in good faith for the purpose of consolidating with other banks shall be exempt from the provisions of this act: *And provided further*, That the assets and liabilities of banks so in liquidation shall be reported by the banks with which they are in process of consolidation.

*Approved, July* 14, 1870.

ACT OF JUNE 6, 1872, CHAPTER 315.

AN ACT TO REDUCE DUTIES ON IMPORTS AND TO REDUCE INTERNAL TAXES, AND FOR OTHER PURPOSES. 37

Taxes on State banks, bankers, &c., to be paid semi-annually.

SEC. 37. That the taxes imposed by section one hundred and ten of the act entitled "An act to provide internal revenue to support the Government, to pay interest on the public debt, and for other purposes," approved June thirtieth, eighteen hundred and sixty-four, as amended by section nine of the act of July thirteenth, eighteen hundred and sixty-six, to reduce internal taxation and to amend the act aforesaid and acts amendatory thereof, upon the deposits, capital, and circulation of banks, or persons, associations, companies, or corporations engaged in the business of banking, shall hereafter be paid semi-annually, on the first day of January and the first day of July; but the same shall be calculated at the rate per month as prescribed by said section, so that the tax for six months shall not be less than the aggregate would be if the said taxes were collected monthly, as prescribed by said section.

What is to be considered as capital.

And the words "capital employed," in said section, shall not include money borrowed or received from day to day, in the usual course of business, from any person not a partner of or interested in the said bank, association, or firm.

Savings banks—

And the exemption from tax, authorized by said section,

of deposits of less than five hundred dollars, made in the name of one person, in associations or companies known as provident institutions, savings banks, savings funds, or savings institutions, is hereby extended to deposits so made of not exceeding two thousand dollars. —deposits to extent of $2,000 exempt.

---

37. By the regulations of the Internal Revenue Bureau, these taxes are to be *assessed* monthly, and returned to the collector as before, but the collector will collect the same only once in six months.

---

## NOTES

### RELATIVE TO TAXATION OF BANKS UNDER EXISTING LAWS.

On and after October 1, 1872, no tax will be imposed on notes, bills of exchange, etc., except "bank checks, drafts, or orders," on which a two-cent stamp will continue to be requisite. (*Act of June* 6, 1872, *chap.* 315, *sec.* 36.)

The tax on dividends expired December 31, 1871. (*Act of July* 14, 1870, *sec.* 15.) The special tax on capital ceased May 1, 1871. (*Same act, sec.* 1.)

United States taxes are now levied on national banks under section 41, act of June 3, 1864, chapter 106. (*See pp.* 125, 160.) And on State banks and bankers under section 110, act of June 30, 1864, chapter 173, and section 37 of the act of June 6, 1872, chapter 315. (*See pp.* 142, 158.)

There is also a law imposing a tax of ten per cent. on notes of "persons, State banks, or State banking associations" *paid out* by national or State banks. This is, virtually, a prohibitory tax. (*See pp.* 145, 146.)

The shares of national banks may be taxed under State authority within a limited extent. (*See p.* 126.)

# REGULATIONS AND INSTRUCTIONS

## IN RELATION TO PAYMENT OF DUTIES BY NATIONAL BANKS.

By the forty-first section of the act entitled "An act to provide a national currency, secured by a pledge of United States bonds and to provide for the redemption and circulation thereof," approved June 3, 1864, it is made the duty of the Treasurer of the United States to prescribe the form for making return, by each national banking association, of the average amount of its notes in circulation, the average amount of its deposits, and the average amount of its capital stock beyond the amount invested in United States bonds, for each half year from and after the first day of January, eighteen hundred and sixty-four. In compliance with this requirement, a form for such return has been prepared, and copies are furnished herewith.

Under the law, a return is to be made within ten days next succeeding the first days of January and July, in each and every year, for the preceding six months.

The penalty for default in making the return within the time fixed is two hundred dollars.

*Items subject to duty.*

Items subject to duty.

The items made subject to duty by the act are circulating notes, deposits and capital stock.

*Dates of commencement of liability to duty.*

When to com mence.

The return of these items from all banks that have before made returns of them will be for the full semi-annual term of 181, 182, or 184 days, as the case may be; and of all banks that have not before made returns of these items, as follows:

Upon circulating notes, from and including the date of their first issue.

Upon deposits, from and including the date of the first deposit received by the bank.

Upon capital stock, from and including the date of the certificate of the Comptroller of the Currency authorizing the commencement of business as a national bank.

*Amount of each item subject to duty.*

The amount of each item subject to duty is the average amount thereof for the half year for which duty is due. **Amount.**

*Rule for ascertaining average amounts.*

I. *For banks making estimates from daily statements of balances.*

Add together the daily balances of the item, from the proper date of the commencement of the liability of the item to duty, (including for each Sunday and holiday the balance of the first preceding business day,) to and including the 30th day of June, or the 31st day of December, as the case may be. This aggregate of daily balances, for the first six months of any year, will be divided by 181, the number of days from January 1 to June 30, except in leap year, when the sum will be divided by 182. The aggregate of daily balances for the last six months of any year will be divided by 184, the number of days from July 1 to December 31. **Average amount, how ascertained.**

II. *For banks making estimates from weekly statements of balances.*

Banks not making daily statements, and which obtain their averages from weekly statements, should add together the weekly balances, including for each day, in any fractional part of a week, one-seventh of the weekly balance next preceding such fractional part. The aggregate of balances for the first six months of any year will be divided by the number of weeks from January 1 to June 30, (25 6-7, or 26, as the case may be.) The aggregate of balances for the last six months will be divided by 26 2-7, the number of weeks from July 1 to December 31.

(Banks having items subject to duty for periods less than a half year, which make their estimates from daily balances, will divide the aggregate of the balances of each item, for the time for which it is liable to duty, by the number of days in the half year; and banks having like items, which make their estimates from weekly balances, by the number of weeks and fractions thereof in the half year.)

The quotients thus found will be the average amounts subject to duty for each six months respectively, and should be entered in the statement under the heading "Dutiable amount," and duty is to be computed thereon at the full semi-annual rate.

*Duty on circulation.*

The duty on circulating notes is one-half of one per centum on the average amount outstanding for the six months. **Duty on circulation.**

11

Liability on this item would commence on the first days of January and July in each and every year, unless a bank had at that time no circulation outstanding, in which case it would commence with the date of the first issue of notes, and terminate on the 30th day of June or the 31st day of December, (as the case may be,) date of commencement and termination both included.

*Duty on deposits.*

On deposits. Under this head must be included the balances on hand, when the books of the bank are closed for the day, which are subject to payment on check or draft, or on return of certificate of deposit, (except deposits made to the credit of the Treasurer of the United States with a national bank depositary,) whether made by individuals, banks, savings banks, bankers, or by States, cities, or towns, whether certificates or certified checks have been issued therefor or not, and, in fact, all descriptions of deposits, except as above excepted, which may be used by the bank, or from which it may derive profits, including deposits upon which the bank pays interest, whether any part of either of such items are directly in the possession of the bank or in the hands of an agent or agents.

The average amount of deposits, including, in the case of a depositary, the average amount to the credit of the Treasurer of the United States from the first days of January and July, (or, in case the bank had not then commenced to receive deposits, from the date of the first deposit,) to the 30th of June, or the 31st of December, (as the case may be,) date of commencement and termination both included, will first be set down in the return. From this average amount, depositaries will be entitled to deduct the average amount on deposit to the credit of the Treasurer of the United States. Upon the remainder, which will be considered the deposits subject to duty, is to be levied a duty of one-fourth of one per centum semi-annually.

*Duty on capital stock.*

On capital stock. The capital stock on which duty is levied is held to be that portion of the paid-up capital stock which is in excess of the United States bonds owned by the bank. The average amount of the paid-up capital from the first days of January or of July (or, in case certificate of authority to commence business had not then been issued by the Comptroller of the Currency, from the date of such certificate) to the 30th day of June or the 31st day of December, date of commencement and termination both included, will first be set down in the return. From this average amount deduction will be made of the average amount of United States bonds, at their face value, owned by the bank, including the bonds on deposit with the Treasurer of the United States as security for circulation, or for other purposes.

The rate of duty on capital stock is one-fourth of one per cent. semi-annually.

The actual capital paid in will be returned, without regard to the amount specially authorized. Thus, an institution should include in the capital liable to duty any increase which has been paid in, although such increase shall not at the date of the return have received the approval of the Comptroller of the Currency.

The term "United States bonds," as used in the act, is construed to mean only coupon or registered bonds, and not any portion of what is considered temporary debt, such as seven and three-tenths treasury notes, certificates of indebtedness, five per cent. notes, compound-interest notes, or temporary loan certificates.

*Payment of duty.*

The duty levied by the section referred to is required by law to be paid to the Treasurer of the United States in the months of January and July in each and every year, in default of which payment provision is made for its collection by the Treasurer out of the interest on securities in his hands, and may be made in any one of the following ways: Payment of duty

1st. By a deposit of the amount of duty to the credit of the Treasurer of the United States, with him, or with any Assistant Treasurer of the United States, or designated depositary, including all national banks, *designated as such*, and including the bank making payment, if a depositary. Triplicate certificates should be issued therefor, the original of which must be forwarded to the Secretary of the Treasury, the duplicate to the Treasurer, and the triplicate held by *the party making the deposit*, in which certificate it should be stated that the deposit is "on account of semi-annual duty."

Depositaries should be careful to distinguish the deposit on this account, as a duty from banks, so as not to confound it with deposits on account of internal-revenue tax, to which latter class it does not belong, and should make the certificate therefor in the name of the depositing bank, and not in the name of one of its officers.

2d. By remittance to this office of the amount of duty in lawful money of the United States, or the notes of national banks; the expense and risk of transmission to be borne by the party remitting.

3d. By draft payable to the order of the Treasurer of the United States, on either of the cities of Washington, New York, Boston, or Philadelphia, to be made payable in the lawful money of the United States, or the notes of national banks.

Payment will not be considered in such cases as having been made until the drafts shall have been collected, and in no case until the semi-annual statement has been examined at this office.

When the draft is collected, certificates of payment of duty will be forwarded by the Treasurer to the bank.

National banks should be careful always to insert the name of the State in which they are located, and to address all correspondence relating to semi-annual duty to the Treasurer of the United States.

# INDEX.

NOTE.—Everything relating to national banking associations is indexed alphabetically under the head of "NATIONAL BANKS."

PAGE.

## N.

PAGE.

www.ingramcontent.com/pod-product-compliance
Lightning Source LLC
LaVergne TN
LVHW011226110826
845150LV00006B/1558
*9781425515904*